HERBERT POPPKE, DENVER

A History of The Volga Relief Society

Emma Schwabenland Haynes

CHILD FEEDING STATION IN ALT DOENNHOF.

A History of The Volga Relief Society

Emma Schwabenland Haynes

Published by
American Historical Society of Germans from Russia
Lincoln, Nebraska
1982

Revised edition printed 1982
Lincoln, Nebraska

First edition printed 1941
Portland, Oregon

ISBN Number: 0-914222-07-4
Library of Congress Catalog
Card Number: 82-072801

Printed by
Augstums Printing Service, Inc.
Lincoln, Nebraska

CONTENTS.

This book is dedicated to the memory
of the thousands of German-Russian
men and women who made the Volga
Relief Society possible.

INTRODUCTION

On August 11, 1921, there was organized in the Zion Congregational Church of Portland, Oregon, a society composed of German people who had emigrated to the United States from Russia. Their purpose in meeting was to raise funds for relatives along the Volga River, who at that time were suffering from one of the most disastrous famines in European history. At this meeting Mr. John W. Miller was chosen president and Mr. George Repp, secretary. Two weeks later, the society voted that Mr. Repp was to be its personal representative in Russia, working under the supervision of the American Relief Administration.

At the same time that this organization came into existence, similar gatherings were held by Volga Germans living in Fresno, California, and in Lincoln, Nebraska. Before very long money was contributed by communities in Colorado, Washington, Montana, Oklahoma, Illinois, Kansas, and many other states in which these people have settled. As a result of their united efforts, more than one million dollars was raised for their unfortunate compatriots in Russia.

The relief work accomplished along the Volga River during the years 1921-1923 has been described by historians as the most outstanding act of charity ever performed by the German-Russian people now living in the United States. Because of the important part that the Volga Relief Society performed in this undertaking, it seems only proper that its history should be written in permanent form; so that in future years the children of today might know something of the truly remarkable achievement of their parents in carrying out the activities of this society. For the benefit of these English-speaking boys and girls a rather lengthy introductory chapter on the history of their ancestors has been included.

On September 11, 1921, a second organization called the Central States Volga Relief Society was formed in Lincoln, Nebraska. All money raised by the people in Portland as well as in Lincoln, was put into a common fund and was distributed through the medium of the American Relief Administration. Because of the close connection in their work, a brief account of the activities of the Lincoln organization will be given. However, the author would like to point out that this story is primary intended to tell the history of the Portland society and of its representative, Mr. George Repp. The period of time covered will be from August, 1921, until November, 1922.

The Author.

Chapter One.

THE STORY OF THE VOLGA GERMANS.

In order to understand the background of the Volga Relief Society it is necessary to devote a few pages to the German-speaking people among whom the work was done.

Before the year 1762, when Catherine the Great gained control of the Russian government, the region along the Volga River south of Simbirsk was inhabited by wild Mongolian tribes called Kalmucks, Bashkirs, Khirghiz, etc. In order to retain a hold over this territory, the government made an attempt to induce Russian peasants to inhabit the area. But the constant danger of attack made this plan unsuccessful, and for a long time it appeared that the district would never be occupied by permanent settlers.

In the first year of her reign, Catherine the Great decided to solve the problem by issuing a manifesto inviting people of all nationalities except Jews to come to Russia and settle there. In this way she hoped that a bulwark against the nomads would be established and that a higher civilization would spread among the Russians. However, the first invitation gained no response whatever, and it was considered necessary to issue a second manifesto on July 22, 1763. In this document the colonists were promised the right to settle in any part of Russia, payment of traveling expenses, freedom of religion, freedom from taxes for thirty years, freedom from military service, and internal self-government.

For several reasons these inducements attracted the greatest attention in Germany. The Seven Years War ended in the year 1763, and as is usually the case, a period of hard times set in. Whole villages lay devastated; soldiers were wandering around looking for work; food was lacking, and poverty existed on all sides. A constant stream of emigration had already begun for Poland, America, and Hungary; and after the appearance of Russian commissioners and agents who were stationed in such cities as Frankfort on the Main, and Ulm and Regensburg in Bavaria, thousands of additional emigrants decided to leave their native homes. Every German district was represented in this exodus, although the largest number of colonists came from Hessen and the Rhineland provinces, which had been particularly hard hit by the war. Other colonists left Thuringia and the large southern provinces of Bavaria and Baden. Many of the descendants of these people later emigrated from Russia to the United States, and after a lapse of one hundred and seventy-five years they can still trace their forefathers back to their original homes in Germany. For example, a family living in Portland, Oregon, knows that an ancestor of theirs, named Conrad Giebelhaus, left the city of Darmstadt in Hessen as an eighteen-year-old boy, and helped to found the colony of Norka in Russia.

Numerous lies and tricks were practised by the agents in their attempts to gain large number of colonists. The Germans were told that the country along the Volga was very similar to the one in which they were living; that the climate was extremely mild, the ground fertile, and the entire region a veritable paradise.

People from many different classes and ranks of society listened to the agents and decided to leave. Farmers, officers, doctors, students, members of the nobility, artists, and craftsmen were all to be found among the emigrants. Besides these, there were also some lazy, shiftless people who thought that they would find an easier mode of life in the faraway steppes.

The emigration finally reached such large proportions that after the year 1766 the rulers of many cities, including Mainz, Trier, Cologne and Frankfurt, all became alarmed and issued decrees forbidding their people to leave the country. After these laws were passed, the commissioners sometimes continued their work in other cities. One of the men, named Facius, set up his headquarters in Büdingen, and his call for emigrants aroused such a tremendous response, that the town soon began to resemble an armed war camp. Many of the young men and women in this group decided to get married before leaving for Russia, and as a result, 375 weddings took place in the Evangelical church of that city between February 24 and July 8, 1766. The names of some of these contracting parties will probably prove interesting to Volga Germans now living in the United States.

Johann Peter Spomer and Anna Margaretha Wagner..........March 10, 1766
Johann Weigand and Appolonie Steiner ....March 11, 1766
Konrad Repp and Anna Margaretha Wallefesch...................March 11, 1766
Johannes Vogel and Anna Martha Kratz.............................March 16, 1766
Johannes Lehr and Margaretha Joss.................................March 18, 1766
Philip Koch and Anna Maria Schneider ....April 4, 1766
Daniel Weygand and Anna Maria Hildebrand.......................April 23, 1766
Johann Heinrich Nazarenus and Anna Maria Koch...............April 23, 1766
Johannes Loos and Anna Maria Sebastian Loos.....................May 3, 1766
Johannes Marquardt and Anna Maria Stephan....................May 11, 1766
Johannes Marquardt and Anna Maria Stephan....................May 11, 1766
Johann Wilhelm Störckel and Maria Catharina Jünger.........May 24, 1766
Christoph Weitzel and Gerdrauth Kessel ....May 24, 1766
Johann Adam Klein and Anna Maria Fischer.......................June 3, 1766
Johann Georg Feuerstein and Agnesa Loch..........................June 12, 1766
Johannes Beckel and Anna Maria Ritzel............................June 15, 1766
Johann Konrad Diehl and Maria Margareta Zimmer (1).......June 23, 1766

It was always customary for the emigrants to meet in a centrally located town, and to travel in a loosely organized band to the northern sea cost. The people from Hessen usually moved from Giessen northward through Kassel and Hildesheim to Lübeck, while those from the area around Würzburg and Nüremberg in Bavaria gathered in Roslau and then came in boats down the river to Hamburg. From this city they would go overland to Lübeck where rough shelters were erected for them, and a strict watch was maintained so that those who were already becoming faint-hearted over the venture would be unable to escape.

While the emigrants were waiting for the boats that took them to Russia, 250 additional marriages took place in Lübeck during the years 1764-1766, when the city was being used as a port of departure for Russia. It can be seen that practically all these people also came from the province of Hessen:

Philip Hinrich Stumpff and Katharina Barbara Hess....January 23, 1766
Valantin Jeckel and Barbara Heitzeräther.... ....April 11, 1766

Johann Heinrich Bartholomo and Elisabeth Branne................May 15, 1766
Johann Jakob Hahn and Anna Magdalena Schneider................May 21, 1766
Nikolaus Spahn and Anna Elisabeth Rieffer................................May 22, 1766
Johann Konrad Popp and Philippina Willman............................May 31, 1766
Johann Meysinger and Eva Popp...May 31, 1766
Johann Kasper Miller and Anna Barbara Schnorr....................June 12, 1766
Johann Ernst Müller and Maria Katharina Finck....................June 13, 1766
Karl Friedrich Lehmann and Anna Christina Plehn................June 16, 1766
Johann Döring and Maria Katharina Müller...............................June 27, 1766
Gottlieb Schlaegel and Kunigunda Walther..............................July 15, 1766
Andreas Müller and Johanna Elisabeth Schnell.......................July 15, 1766
Johann Heinrich Schmidt and Eva Zimmermann......................July 22, 1766
Konrad Kern and Maria Amalia Peter...July 29, 1766
Johann Kaspar Geist and Katharina Volbing.......................August 22, 1768
Johann Hohnstein and Anna Maria Reichert (2)............September 13, 1766

Before embarking, each person was given sixteen
shillings with which to buy food for the trip, and the
poorest and most ragged were given new clothing.
Bread, zwieback, pickled meat, wine, and French brandy
were stored away in the hold. After everything was in
readiness, the order to sail was given.

Ordinarily this trip from Lübeck to Kronstadt in
Russia could have been made in ten days, but some un-
scrupulous captains purposely lengthened the journey
in order to sell their provisions at many times the normal price. After their arrival in Kronstadt, the German immigrants were driven to the citv of Oranien-
baum nearby, where they took an oath of allegiance to
the empress. It was here that the colonists suffered
their first big disillusionment. One of the main privileges of Catharine's manifesto had been the right of
the settlers to live wherever they pleased, but with the
exception of a few craftsmen who were allowed to remain in Petrograd, all of the other men and women
were told that they would have to make their homes
along the Volga River.

The next stage of the journey to Petrograd was covered either by land or by sea. In the capitol city each
individual was again provided with money for his traveling expenses, and soldiers were assigned for the rest
of the journey, which ordinarily took a year to complete. The route that was followed led them through
Novgorod, Waldai and Tver, and then either by land
over Moscow and Pensa, or by boat down the Volga to
Saratov.

(A) See WALTERS

The historians tell us that winter set in after the parties left Novgorod, and that they found it necessary to spend the coldest months of the year in the Russian villages along the way. One of the things that amazed them very much was that the peasants with whom they stayed kept their cattle, chickens, sheep and even pigs, under the same roof with them. The food that they were offered in these crowded Russian houses was also extremely unappetizing to the German men and women, who were accustomed to having fresh butter, eggs, meat etc.

During these winter months, priests and ministers appeared from time to time in order to comfort the sick, bury the dead, baptize new-born children, and to perform marriage ceremonies. In the spring the journey continued, and finally after "many hardships, disappointments, and hunger, cold, and sickness" the first settlers reached the city of Saratov. (3).

The greatest disappointment, however, came when the colonists were driven in wagons out to the open steppes which were to be their future homes. When they left Germany, they had been told that everything would be in readiness for them in Russia: houses would be found built, farm implements and livestock on hand, and the land marked out. But all their dreams of a "Paradise" were suddenly shattered. In some places lean-tos had been constructed and the land surveyed, but in other regions absolutely nothing had been done.

One colonists remarks, "We looked at each other with frightened expressions. We were in a wilderness without even a tree. Nothing was to be seen except the endless dry grass of the steppes."

In order to protect themselves against the cold winter which they knew would come, the people began to build partly-underground huts in the manner of the Tartars. Such shelters were called "Semlinken" and were large enough for three or four families, although the crowded conditions and lack of ventilation made them a far from desirable mode of existence.

During the suceeding years, immigrants continued to come and establish colonies, so that in 1773 there were 104 villages with a total population of 27,000 people. The historian Beratz gives us the following information on the date of settlement and the number of inhabitants that each colony had in the year 1773:

Dobrinka	June 29, 1764	353 inhabitants
Beideck	August 10, 1764	360 inhabitants
Balzer	August 28, 1765	479 inhabitants
Straub	May 12, 1767	209 inhabitants
Dinkel	May 12, 1767	179 inhabitants
Warenburg	May 12, 1767	579 inhabitants
Frank	May 16, 1767	525 inhabitants
Kukkus	June 26, 1767	181 inhabitants
Huck	July 1, 1767	380 inhabitants
Grimm	July 1, 1767	769 inhabitants
Laub	July 12, 1767	219 inhabitants
Norka	August 15, 1767	957 inhabitants

All of the first colonists were located or the west bank of the Volga, called the "Berg" or hilly side; but in 1765 villages were founded on the eastern shore as well. Dobrinka was the oldest settlement, and Norka with its 957 people was the largest. Four colonies were established in the year 1764; 11 in 1765; 20 in 1766, and 68 in 1767. Of these settlements, 46 were on the Bergseite of the Volga and 59 were on the opposite side, called the meadow or "Wiesenseite." (5).

Every family, no matter what the size, could claim thirty dessiatines of land, (6) five of which were to be used for a house and garden and the other twenty-five for farming purposes. However, the twenty-five dessiatines were not regarded as a permanent possession, and when a person left the colony, his land simply returned to the commune or "Gemeinde." Then at the beginning of the nineteenth century, the Russian "Mir System" was introduced, according to which the soil was periodically re-divided by lot among all male souls, each of whom was called a "dusch."

During these early years the German colonists suffered a great many hardships. The poor living conditions have already been mentioned. In addition there was a scarcity of food, bad water, few doctors, and intensely cold winters. As a result of all these factors, it is not surprising to read that a typhus-like fever caused the death of thousands of people.

We must also remember that the German settlers were not predominantly farmers. Many of them had hoped to earn their living in the Russian cities and had been forced to take up agriculture against their will. Beratz tells us, "Here stood a tailor; there a wigmaker; neither of them had ever harnessed a horse, not to mention worked in the fields, but nevertheless they were given an old Kalmuck horse, and a few pieces of lumber with which to make a plow and a wagon, and were calmly told to get to work." (7).

Further difficulties were caused by the mis-government of the Russian directors, and constant danger of attacks from the various nomadic tribes. The Kalmucks usually restricted themselves to horse-stealing and robbery, but the Bashkirs and particularly the Khirghiz would attack and burn villages, steal everything in sight, and then sell the inhabitants into slavery. The settlements on the east or Wiesenseite suffered particularly in this way. Four colonies were completely destroyed in 1774, and two years later the Catholic village of Marienthal was attacked and 300 inhabitants were carried away into slavery. It is estimated that at least 1,200 people were taken captive in this manner. Many of the women and children were then sold into the harems of wealthy Mohamedans in countries under the control of Turkey.

Pugachev's rebellion which took place between the years 1773-1775 also caused untold suffering for the German people. This bold Cossack with his robber band swept like a tornado over the Volga colonies, stealing everything in sight. Sick people were thrown out of their beds; women and children driven from their homes; houses and barns burned, and the cattle driven away.

As a result of all these disasters, we hear that many of the colonists longed to return to their German homes. Several groups even set out with this purpose in mind, but only a few managed to escape, and the rest were forcibly brought back by Cossacks.

However, as time went on, conditions became more peaceful, and after a younger generation grew up, the German people gradually reconciled themselves to their life in Russia. The professional and educated gave up all hopes of being anything except farmers, and in many cases were even an example in diligence to other members of the community. The primitive Russian plows and sickles were now exchanged for better ones. Roomy houses were built, water mills constructed, new industries introduced, and more honest officials came to rule, so that eventually the colonists even began to consider themselves fortunate and happy.

During the ensuing years the German villages continued to grow and prosper. The population increased from the original 27,000 to 552,207 in the year 1910. At that time the people were divided in the following religious groups:

Evangelical Protestants	435,667
Catholics	112,876
Sarepta Moravians	2,465
Mennonites	1,207

552,207

Because of the fact that the farming land of a village was held in common, and periodically re-divided among all the men and male children, the number of dessiatines per person began to rapidly decrease. For example, in the year 1816 there were 10.4 dessiatines per "dusch", but in 1857 only 3.2 dessiatines. For this reason the Russian government gave the German people an additional 250,000 dessiatines of land which lay east of the original Wiesenseite colonies. This land was much less fertile than the first grant had been, and in order to induce a sufficient number of the families to leave their homes, they were each given 100 rubles and were told that they would not be required to pay any taxes for ten years. These colonies often took the name of the village from which they came, and thus we hear of Neu Warenburg, Neu Norka, Neu Schilling, etc. The organization of these new villages continued from 1842 to 1909. During this period 91 colonies were established, although ten of them consisted of Mennonites from the Black Sea region. Consequently, there were approximately 190 German communities along the Volga at the outbreak of the World War. (9).

When one considers how rapidly immigrants become

Americanized in the United States, it seems amazing
that during this period of 150 years the colonies remained so intrinsically German. Very few of the people even learned to speak the Russian language. They
lived in compact German villages; they inter-married
only with Germans; their schools were conducted in
German, and their Lutheran and Reformed pastors
preached sermons in German. After their arrival in
Russia they made very little progress in industry and
agriculture. It is even possible that there was some re-
trogression in their intellectual life, but at all times
the greater cleanliness of the women, and the greater
industry of the men kept them separated from their
Russian neighbors.

The principal crops of the lower Volga are grains of
all kinds, but particularly wheat and rye. Since very
little fertilizer was used, the average yield per acre was
much less than what it is in the United States. Of the
two grains, the rye was more often kept for home use
while the wheat was shipped away. The cattle industry was never of great importance, although each
household usually possessed sufficient chickens, sheep,
pigs, and four to eight cows and horses for its own use.
Oxen were kept for field work, and camels were sometimes used as a means of transportation. The farming
land of the colonists often lay from fifteen to twenty-
five "versts" away from the village, (10) and during the
spring plowing and the harvest season a general exodus
would take place to the fields where the people would
stay day and night until the work was done. Thresh-
ing was accomplished by means of a large six-cornered
stone pulled by two horses walking around in a circle,
although some machinery was later introduced.

After the year 1906 the Stolypin Land Reform Bills
made it possible for the villages to decide for themselves if they wanted to introduce private property. In
many of the colonies the advantages of the new method
were immediately seen and the change made, but in
other places the people preferred to use the old-fashion-
ed Mir System, and continued to live in a patriarchal
fashion with the father of the family wielding complete
authority over his sons. In such cases a single house-

hold often consisted of twenty-five or thirty people, since even the married sons continued to live at home with their wives and children.

Apart from agriculture, the greatest industry on the Volga was the manufacture of grain into flour. This occupation lay almost entirely in the hands of German manufacturers and merchants, many of whom owned large mills in Saratov and other cities, from which they sent their flour to the Baltic ports for trans-shipment to foreign countries of the entire world.

The spinning and weaving industries were also of great importance, particularly on the Bergseite. This work was usually done by the people in their homes during the long winter months. The finished cloth was then either put aside for private use, or else sold to a middleman and the money used in payment of the yearly taxes.

The city of Marxstadt on the Wiesenseite had factories making farm machinery, hats, baskets, felt articles, as well as steam mills, saw mills, and foundries. In Balzer on the Bergseite mention is also made of steam mills, a weaving factory, four stocking factories, seventeen tanneries, eight wagon factories, etc. (11).

With regard to the religious and educational life of the colonies, it should be said that there was always a shortage of properly-trained pastors and school teachers. Many of the ministers had three to six colonies in their parish, with a total population of fifteen to twenty thousand people. The parsonage was situated in the largest village of the parish, and from there the pastor would go alternately to the other colonies.

In the center of the village a square was laid out for the white-painted church and bell tower, from which a nightly Angelus was rung. Whenever an inhabitant of the community died, it was customary for the bell-ringer to designate by the first few peals whether the person was a man, woman, or child, and then to toll out his age. The bells were also used in case of a fire, and were rung steadily on nights when a blizzard was raging in order to designate to possible wanderers where the village was located. In addition to these two buildings, the church square contained the schoolhouse and a parsonage, if the colony was large enough to have one.

As time went on, interest in education lessened to a very great extent in the Volga villages, and it became customary to choose teachers whose chief qualification consisted of a willingness to serve for a small amount of money. In some cases the school teacher himself had difficulty in reading and writing, and as he usually had hundreds of children under his care, it is easy to assume that he was not able to teach them a great deal. Many of the pastors tried to get laws passed which would better the educational conditions of their parish, but as a whole, school rooms remained crowded and the instruction consisted primarily of learning to read the Bible and Catechism and of memorizing church songs out of the "Volga Gesangbuch."

An ordinary German-Russian house on the Volga was of white painted wood, covered with straw or tin; but the parsonage and the homes of the wealthier people were of stone or brick. The architecture showed a strong Russian influence, but inside the house German furniture, pictures and even kitchen utensils predominated. The only two exceptions to this rule were the Russian samovar, and the primitive built-in oven over which the family cooking was done. The most interesting piece of furniture was the extremely high bed, with its feather quilts, and crocheted spread, pillow slips, and "Vorhang." In front of the houses long benches were usually placed. Here the family would sit in the evening enjoying the fresh air and discussing the affairs of the day with their friends.

When one considers that the German settlers had become reasonably satisfied with this life which has just been described, it may seem surprising that so many of them emigrated to the United States, Canada, and South America between the years 1874 and 1914. In order to understand the background of this great exodus, it is necessary to refer again to Catherine's Manifesto.

Two of the most important sections of this document had been the right of the colonists to govern themselves, and the promise that they would not have to serve in the Russian army. These provisions were at first kept, but reactionary czars later came to the throne, and after the year 1860 a series of laws were passed withdrawing many of the former privileges of self-government. In addition, the Educational Law of 1890 commanded that a Russian teacher be placed in every German school. However, the indignation aroused by these two measures was very mild when compared with the peoples reaction to a ukase of June 4, 1871, which made military training compulsory in the colonies. After the first young men were called into the army, stories of their ill-treatment began to spread along the Volga, and as result, thousands of twenty-year-old boys decided to leave the country.

In addition to the influence of the Military Law, many people emigrated from Russia because of the bad economic conditions in their villages, due to the lack of adequate land and the crop failures in 1879-1880 and between 1890-1893. As a further incentive, the advertisements of American railroad companies, promising jobs to all newcomers, began to circulate among the German colonies; and in many cases the passage money to the United States was even sent by friends and relatives who had saved it out of their first earnings in the new world. The Russo-Japanese War of 1904-1905 should also be mentioned as an important factor in inducing many of the more recent immigrants to come to America.

Nevertheless, it would appear that the Military Law of 1871 was the chief reason why the earliest colonists left. Some emissaries were first sent to the United States to search for a suitable place of settlement. The reports of these men were so satisfactory that in 1874 a group of people from both the Berg and Wiesenseite left their homes and settled in Nebraska and Kansas. A second group came in the fall of the same year to Arkansas, and a few months later a third group settled in Iowa. Neither of these last two states proved very popular, however, and before very long, Nebraska became the chief distributing center for thousands of Volga Germans. The towns of Sutton, Lincoln, and Hastings were especially important in this connection.

During these early years, the wealthier emigrants established themselves on farms, but the large majority of less prosperous ones first worked on construction gangs for the Burlington and other railroads. Because of their unusual thrift, many of them saved enough money to purchase homes in the places in which they were stationed. Even today it is amazing to notice how many German-Russians live in the communities between Lincoln, Nebraska, and Denver, Colorado, through which the Burlington Railroad passes. After 1900 the sugar beet industry of northern Colorado caused many of the first settlers to leave Nebraska and Kansas for such towns as Greeley, Loveland, Fort Morgan, Windsor, etc. Another large settlement of Volga Germans is found in and around Fresno, California. These people came primarily from the Wiesenseite between the years 1886 and 1914 and have helped to make the San Joaquin Valley famous for its beautiful vineyards and fruit orchards.

In 1882 a few Volga Germans from Iowa and Nebraska moved to Portland, Oregon, although the great majority of the people arrived between 1890-1895. At the present time they are found in practically every occupation and profession. In the state of Washington they are often the possessors of immense wheat ranches, particularly in the Big Bend district; and in addition to the cities already mentioned, large numbers have also settled in Chicago, Illinois; Saginaw, Michigan; Billings, Montana, Sheboygan, Wisconsin; and many towns in Kansas, Oklahoma, and other middle western states. It is estimated that approximately fifty per cent are engaged in agriculture and the other fifty per cent in industry. (12).

Because of the steady stream of emigration from Russia, and the rapid increase of the population in America, we know that at least 120,000 Volga Germans of the first and second generation were living in the United States in the year 1920. Richard Sallet in his book on German-Russian settlements in America arrives at this figure by an examination of the census returns for that year, but it would be reasonable to suppose that the actual number was even higher, since many of the immigrants had already lost contact with their national group. Mr. Sallet lists the states in which they had settled as follows: (13).

	Prot.	Cath.
California	8,000	....
Colorado	16,000	3,500
Idaho	800	....
Illinois	6,900	1,000
Iowa	500	500
Kansas	9,750	9,000
Ohio	1,000	700
Michigan	6,500	50
Minnesota	750	....
Missouri	500	500
Montana	4,500	266
Nebraska	19,000	....
North Dakota	500	85
Oklahoma	4,000	30
Oregon	3,750	1,000
South Dakota	600	37
Texas	500	....
Washington	5,000	375
Wisconsin	7,300	700
Wyoming	1,900	....
Other States	2,000	1,000
	99,750	18,743

According to these figures, the three states having the greatest number of Protestant and Catholic Volga Germans are Colorado, Nebraska, and Kansas. In addition to these two groups there are also German-Russian Mennonites living primarily in Kansas, although the largest number of people belonging to this denomination come from the Black Sea area in southern Russia.

In many of the communities in which Volga Germans live, the older people still congregate in one section of town, such as the district around F Street in Lincoln, Nebraska; Kirk Street in Fresno, California; and N. E. 7th Avenue in Portland, Oregon. The younger people, however, are inter-marrying with other racial groups and are moving into more modern residential districts, where their children hear nothing but the English language and the parents themselves have forgotten how to speak German.

Because of the fact that upon their arrival in America the Volga Germans felt no complete allegiance to either Germany or Russia, it was very easy for them to break off all European political ties and to develop a feeling of loyalty to the United States. In addition, their honesty, hospitality, law-abiding spirit, and unusual thrift and industry have made them a definite asset to every community in which they have settled.

The satisfaction that the Volga Germans felt in their newly-acquired country was even increased after the outbreak of the European war in 1914. Since Russia and Germany were fighting on opposite sides, every foreigner speaking the enemy language was looked upon with suspicion in these two countries. The first group to suffer were the Wolhynien and Polish Germans who lived in the western part of Russia. On February 2, 1915, they were commanded to sell all their possessions and to migrate eastward. Although a liquidation period of ten months was supposed to elapse, historians tell us that in some regions the inhabitants were merely given a twenty-four hour notice. (14).

In December of the same year a second law was passed depriving the Germans of Finland, the Baltic states, and those living in the Caucasian and Black Sea region of the right to hold land. In February, 1917, a similar measure was intended for the Volga Germans, but the March Revolution occurred just in time to prevent this last law from being put into effect. Hopes for a more peaceful existence now spread through the colonies, and in April a great colonial congress was held in Saratov. At this meeting the German-Russians expressed a desire for self-government and asked to be recognized by the Kerensky government.

However, the summer of 1917 was merely a brief respite before the outbreak of even greater disasters. In November the communist party under the leadership of Lenin gained control of the government, and almost immediately repercussions of this act were felt along the Volga. The first colony to be attacked by the Red Guards was the city of Balzer, which was seized in December of 1917. From that time on the entire Volga Valley became a battlefield for roving bands of soldiers, criminal and unprincipled ruffians, whose attacks on the civilian population and seizure of food, clothing, livestock, and wealth kept the inhabitants of the villages in constant terror. One morning at five o'clock the town of Katharinenstadt was besieged by such a mob consisting of about one hundred men, including Czech and Latvian as well as Russian soldiers. The members of the church council and all the wealthy inhabitants of the city were seized and imprisoned. A demand was then made that the colony "contribute" two million rubles to the marauders, and the people were told that the soldiers would remain in the village until this sum was handed over to them. In the meantime the prisoners were subjected to unmerciful persecution, until their resistance was completely broken and they agreed to relinquish a large sum of money in return for their freedom.

Another colony to suffer was Schaffhausen which was attacked by the Red Guards on Sunday morning of April 7, 1918, while most of the inhabitants were in church. Nevertheless, the people resisted so bravely that they were able to disarm the mob and drive it out of town. In the fighting nineteen men lost their lives. The Germans knew that the soldiers would return and immediately warned the four neighboring villages of what had happened. They also organized a local militia for self-protection, and since there were not enough guns for everyone, many of the men armed themselves with pitchforks, scythes, axes, etc.

Just as they expected, Schaffhausen was re-visited that very night, but because of the preparation that had been made, the communists were again defeated. They then offered a truce, and the German people agreed to lay down their arms. As soon as this was done, a much larger band of Red Guards completely plundered the unsuspecting village, killed many of its inhabitants arrested its leaders, and drove off a large part of its livestock. (15).

The story of what occurred in Katharinenstadt and Schaffhausen could be repeated for Dobrinka, Zürich, Warenburg, Norka and innumerable other colonies on both sides of the river. In the streets of Saratov artillery battles took place between Bolsheviks, Anarchists, Front soldiers, and members of the Social Revolutionary party. For weeks at a time the inhabitants were afraid to leave their homes, and cowered behind locked doors or in their cellars. Many of the wealthiest people feared for their lives, and fled to small German villages where they attempted to hide in the homes of their friends. As Schleuning tells us, "No house, no horse, no land, no person's life was safe." (16).

Because of the resulting terror, all activity seemed to come to a stand-still. The few boats that remained on the Volga were used to transport soldiers and ammunition. People were often afraid to work alone in their fields, and even when they did harvest their crops, the constant "contributions" and "requisitions" deprived them of all incentive for future labor. Any village which resisted the Bolsheviks was treated with special severity, and was likely to lose not only its grain and livestock but to have all men and boys of military age taken off as well.

During the ensuing year a great deal of fighting also took place between the Reds and the so-called Whites. This latter army included many Cossack soldiers, who proceeded to steal everything that the Bolsheviks had failed to carry away. The Bergseite towns especially lay in this zone of battle, and some of the German villages passed back and forth as many as seven different times until the communists won their final victories in the summer of 1919.

As soon as the news of the Bolshevik success spread, hundreds of Germans who had fought against them tried to disguise themselves and flee from their homes before the arrival of their enemies. The cities of Kamyschin and Tzaritzin were soon full of such frightened refugees vainly trying to find boats in which they could escape down the Volga. Because of this long Civil War with its numerous executions, deaths from fighting, and partial evacuation, it is not surprising to read that the population of the German colonies decreased from 600,000 to 431,000 between the years 1914 and 1920. (17).

The harvest of 1919 was unusually good, but the Wiesenseite villages were the only ones that could take advantage of it. Such Bergseite colonies as Grimm, Balzer, Messer and Franzosen, which were the scene of especially severe battles, were naturally prevented from carrying on their work in a normal fashion. However, in all the villages the requisitions of large amounts of grain continued. The peasants were promised that they would be given manufactured articles in exchange for their contributions, but when such supplies failed to arrive, they became disgusted and began to put smaller amounts of land under cultivation. As a result of all of these conditions there was a definite crop shortage in 1920, but the demands of the tax collectors remained unmercifully high.

But the greatest disaster of all was yet to come. In 1921 there arrived a world-wide drought which was especially severe along the Volga River. Ordinarily a large amount of grain was kept on hand for such an emergency, but since it had all been seized in the preceding years, deaths from starvation immediately began to take place. As soon as they realized how serious the food shortage had become, thousands of desperate Germans fled from their villages towards the western borders of Russia, so that between 1920-1921 there was a further decrease of 72,000 people in the Volga colonies. (18). Some of the other settlers wrote pitiful letters to friends and relatives in America telling that unless help came to them soon, they would all die of starvation and disease. The Soviet government at first refused to acknowledge the urgency of the situation, but finally, on July 13, Maxim Gorki was given permission to tell of the crop failure and to ask the world to help save millions of Russians from starvation. His appeal, which appeared in the press on July 23, was addressed "To All honest People" and ended with the hope that the European and American people would send bread and medicine to Russia as soon as possible. (19).

Since no foreign newspaper correspondents were

then allowed in Russia, the news of an approaching famine came as a great surprise to many Americans. For example, in issues of "Literary Digest" of 1921 no mention is made of a food shortage until the August 6 number, when an article appeared under the heading, "Millions Starving in Lenin's Paradise of Atheism." The article told that:

> "Millions of hungry Russian peasants are being driven from their parched farms to the wretched cities in search of food ... The greatest part of these must die of hunger. In those regions which normally produce most breadstuffs, all grain is now annihilated by drought. Epidemics are following in the wake of famine. Immediate help on a large scale is imperative."

In the same article Walter Duranty, a correspondent for the "New York Times" is said to have cabled:

> "This is a national disaster on a scale the modern world has never known outside of China. ... Even in Moscow the food supply is terribly curtailed. Sal ed herring and thin gruel of millet, wheat, and oats are the only food the majority has tasted since early spring. The regions worst afflicted by drought present a dreadful picture. Beneath a sky of steel gray the fields are parched and the wheat withered on the stalk. In the ground long fissures have appeared, until it seems to the terrified peasants that the earth herself is opening her mouth to swallow them. Since March no rain has fallen. Wells and springs have dried up until there is no water for man or beast."

Herbert Hoover is then quoted as saying that if all American prisoners were set free, and if the Soviet goverment agreed not to interfere with the distribution of food and to provide free transportation of supplies, the American Relief Administration would be willing to furnish food, clothing and medical supplies to 1,000,000 children in Russia as rapidly as their organization could be effected. (20).

This particular article was seen by Mr. and Mrs. George Repp of Portland, Oregon, who were subscribers of the "Literary Digest" at the time. They knew that letters had been arriving in Portland begging the German-Russians of that city to come to the help of their relatives along the Volga, and the thought came to Mr. and Mrs. Repp that it might be possible for an organization to send food to the German colonies under the supervision of the American Relief Administration. This plan was discussed with Mrs. Repp's brother, Mr. John W. Miller, who considered it an excellent suggestion, and in this way the idea of organizing a Volga Relief Society came into being.

FOOTNOTES

1. Hoffmann, Hermann "Auswanderung nach Russland im Jahre 1766." Mitteilungen der hessischen familiengeschichtlichen Vereinigung. Darmstadt, January 1927. pp. 109-122.
2. Jahrbuch des Deutschtums im Ausland 1939. "Der Wanderweg der Russlanddeutschen." Deutsches Ausland Institut. Stuttgart, 1939. pp. 111-116.
3. Beratz, Gottlieb. Die deutschen Kolonien an der unteren Wolga in ihrer Entstehung und ersten Entwicklung. Saratow: H. Schellhorn und Co., 1915. p. 55.
4. Bonwetsch, Gerhard. Geschichte der deutschen Kolonien an der Wolga. Stuttgart: Verlag von J. Engelhorns Nachf., 1919. p. 33.
5. Beratz, op. cit., pp. 304-311.
6. One dessiatine is 2.170 acres.
7. Beratz, op. cit., p. 138.
8. Bonwetsch, op. cit., p. 122.
9. Ibid., pp. 121-122.
10. A verst is two-thirds of a mile.
11. Schleuning, J. Die deutschen Kolonien im Wolgagebiet. Portland, Oregon, 1921. pp. 11-12.
12. Sallet, Richard. "Russlanddeutsche Siedlungen in den Vereinigten Staaten." Vol. XXXI of Jahrbuch der Deutsch- Amerikanischen Historischen Gesellschaft von Illinois. Chicago, Ill.: The University of Chicago Press, 1931. p. 82.
13. Ibid., p. 108.
14. Schleuning, Johannes. Aus tiefster Not. Berlin, 1922. p. 13.
15. Ibid., pp. 29-35.
16. Ibid., p. 83.
17. Bonwetsch, op. cit., pp. 122-123. Golder, Frank and Lincoln Hutchinson, On the Trail of the Russian Famine. Stanford University, California: Stanford University Press, 1927. p. 88.
18. Golder and Hutchinson, op. cit., p. 88.
19. Fisher, H. H. The Famine in Soviet Russia 1919-1923. New York: The McMillan Company, 1927. p. 52.
20. Literary Digest, August 6, 1921, p. 32.

Note: Much of the material in this chapter is taken from a Master's Thesis, German-Russians on the Volga and in the United States, written by the author in 1929.

JOHN W. MILLER
President Volga Relief Society

GEORGE REPP
Representative in Russia.

Chapter Two.

THE ORGANIZATION OF VOLGA RELIEF SOCIETIES.

Before meeting with the Volga Germans living in Portland, Oregon, Mr. Miller considered it advisable to get in touch with Herbert Hoover's organization and find out if it was possible to work through the American Relief Administration. As a result, the following night letter was sent on August 8. (1).

European Relief Committee,
42 Broadway, New York City.

There are approximately fifteen hundred people in Portland that came from German colonies located in Russia near city of Saratov along Volga River. These people are anxious to help get food into that stricken district of Russia. They have received letters from relatives appealing for help. Will you be good enough to wire us how to proceed. That is, can we send money to you and designate that it is to be spent for food for a certain colony. Also have you any idea when relief work and food distribution will begin in Russia. There will be a mass meeting Thursday evening among our people and a regular relief committee organized for German speaking colonies in Russia. We would like very much have your reply by then giving us all information you can that may help in the organization. Have hopes extending work of this committee to other places where our people are located in California, Washington, Idaho, Montana, Colorado, Dakotas, Nebraska, Iowa, and Kansas. We figure that there are in the United States approximately hundred thousand people interested in these German speaking colonies along the Volga River and that good work can be done with proper help from reliable source like yourselves. Would it be possible for us to send an American citizen of our people into these colonies in Russia through your committee. That is, be indorsed by you or even sent by you as one of your workers so that he would have proper protection.

JOHN W. MILLER.

An answer to this telegram came on the following day from Edgar Rickard of the American Relief Administration who wrote:

John W. Miller, Portland.

Answering your wire this date we are prepared with personnel and supplies enter Russia moment satisfactory agreement reached with Soviet authorities. Operation will be confined to childfeeding. Impossible determine before actual entry Russia precise need or extent operations and will wire you fully moment we have results survey of conditions. We will gladly accept contributions for general childfeeding but we would not be warranted in accepting cash contributions for any specific locality until scope of our activity more definitely determined.

AMERICAN RELIEF ADMINISTRATION.

Since Mr. Rickard had failed to answer the question whether it would be possible for an American citizen of German-Russian descent to go to the Volga colonies, a lengthy letter was then written by Mr. Miller amplifying his previous telegram and asking for further advise in case the A. R. A. failed to enter the section of Russia in which the Volga colonies were located.

Two days later, on August 11, about one hundred men who were interested in the project gathered in the Zion Congregational Church of Portland, and voted to organize a relief society. The officers elected were: John W. Miller, president; David Hilderman, vice-president; George Repp, secretary; and John H. Krieger, treasurer, although Mr. Krieger resigned in the next meeting and was replaced by Mr. Gottfried Geist. George Repp made the motion that the organization should be called the Volga Relief Society. It was also decided that all gatherings should open and close with prayer and that a second mass meeting was to take place on the following Thursday night.

The enthusiastic response of the Portland people to the news that an organization had been perfected was far greater than anyone could have believed possible. Throughout the following days the newly-elected leaders were constantly being stopped by Volga German men and women who expressed their happiness in the creation of the society. In view of the seriousness of the crisis that existed in Russia, all religious and personal differences were forgotten, and people of all denominations and from all colonies showed a spirit of harmony and co-operation that was to remain truly remarkable. The future success of the Volga Relief Society can be explained to a great extent by the splendid loyalty of its members, which became an example for Volga Germans in many other communities of the States.

Mention should also be made of the wonderful help given by the pastors of the various churches. Rev. H. Hagelganz, Rev. George Zocher, and Rev. John H. Hopp, who had Congregational denominations, Rev. Peter Yost of the Brethren Church, and Rev. Jacob Hergert, an Evangelical pastor, all attended the union meetings, and their unfailing encouragement, advice, and support were of inestimable value to the society. The hymn "Was kann es schönres geben, und was kann seliger sein", which was always sung at the beginning of all meetings, truly expressed the spirit of the Portland people.

During the ensuing week the news of the Russian famine continued to be one of the big topics in all American newspapers and in many periodicals. At least a dozen foreign correspondents left immediately for Riga, Latvia, where negotiations were going on between Maxim Litivinov and Walter Lyman Brown of the A. R. A.'s London office. At this time many refugees were fleeing across the Russian border into Latvia and bringing with them horrible tales of the despair and suffering they had seen. One of the dispatches cabled back to the United States told of "scores of people being crushed to death in their efforts to board railroad trains, of people staggering after departing trains crying: "In the name of God give us bread, for we are dying." Another story told that 6,000,000 ragged peasants were marching on Moscow, and that the vanguard had entered one city, looted all the stores and warehouses, seized every morsel of food, and even killed and devoured the horses belonging to the city's fire department. (2) Some of these accounts were later said to have been exaggerated, but they all helped to make Americans realize that there was an urgent need for immediate assistance in Russia.

On August 20 an agreement was signed by Mr. Litivinov in which the Soviet government made the following promises.

> 1. That American representatives of the Relief Administration should be given full liberty to come and go and move about Russia.

2. That these members should be allowed to organize
the necessary local committees with local assistance free
from governmental interference.

3. That they should be given free transportation of imported supplies with priority over other traffic; that the
authorities should assign necessary buildings and equip-
ment and fuel free of charge.

4. That in addition to the imported food, clothing, and
medicines, the children and sick should be given the same
rations of such local supplies as were given to the rest
of the population.

5. That the Relief Administration would have the assurance of non-interference of the Government with the liber-
ty of all of its members. (3).

In return, the A. R. A. agreed to feed children and
adults in the famine area to the best of its ability and
gave formal assurances that the American personnel
would not participate in political questions.

In the meantime a second mass meeting of the Volga Relief Society was held on August 18 under the
chairmanship of Mr. John W. Miller. Mr. Miller had
been born in this country and always experienced a
certain amount of difficulty in conducting a meeting in
the German language. His standard joke on such oc-
casions was that he must be an unusually well-educated
man because he could speak English, a little German,
the Norkerish dialect of his parents, and "Kauder-
welsh" or a mixture of all three.

At this gathering the first donations for relief work
were made. It was stated that the money could either
be ear-marked for a specific colony in Russia or else be
given to a General Fund for feeding in the villages
where it would be most needed. This latter suggestion
was made by Rev. Peter Yost and was to prove of tremendous value in saving the lives of people in the
poorer villages for which inadequate provision had been
made. When the evening came to a close, $6,075.00 had
been pledged by the members of the audience. The individual sums ranged from $25.00 to $200.00 and were
designated for twenty different colonies along the Volga. However, since a large proportion of the German-

— 36 —

Russian people living in Portland came from the colony of Norka, this particular village naturally received the greatest donations.

The question of sending a man to Russia was still unsettled on the night of August 18. The A. R. A. seemed reluctant to add an inexperienced worker to their staff, and stated that they had been obliged to refuse such requests in the past. Mr. Miller then sent a telegram pointing out that the Volga Relief Society would pay any expenses which such an act involved, and that the sending of a personal representative would add immeasurably to the amount of money that would be contributed. Three days later a wire was received from Mr. Rickard saying there was no further objection to the sending of a representative provided it was understood that the nominee met the approval of the A. R. A. and would be subject to the same discipline as other American workers in Russia.

Mr. Miller then proceeded to carry out the plans expressed in his first telegram to New York—of forming a national organization of all Volga Germans. In order to get in touch with people in other parts of the United States, a circular letter was sent on August 23 to the ministers of every German Congregational church in the United States and Canada, since it is well known that practically all German-speaking members of this denomination come from Russia. This was not done with the purpose of making the Volga Relief Society a Congregational organization, but merely to form the nucleus of a mailing list which later included people and pastors of many different denominations and religious sects. However, it should be pointed out that as a whole, the Mennonites and Catholics from the Volga region formed their own relief organizations, and played a relatively small part in the Portland society; so that most of the money was contributed by members of such Protestant churches as the Congregational, Lutheran, and Evangelical to which the largest number of Volga Germans belong.

The story of the organization of the Volga Relief Society and the suggestion that branch societies be formed in other parts of the United States was also sent to the various newspapers with German-Russian subscribers. The two most important of these were the "Dakota Freie Presse" published in New Ulm, Minn., and the "Welt Post" of Lincoln, Nebraska. Other papers included the "Nachrichten" in Portland, Oregon, the "California Post" in Fresno, and the "Kirchenbote", published for German Congregationalists. All of these periodicals devoted a large part of their space to news from the Volga villages. In this way they were of tremendous help in keeping the people informed of the latest development in the famine area.

On the night of August 25 the most important task facing the members of the Relief Society was the choosing of their Russian representative. When the president anounced that nominations were in order, Mr. Henry Hopp arose and stated that in his opinion there was only one person in Portland whose business experience and ability made it possible for him to carry out this task in a completely satisfactory manner, and that that person was their own secretary, George Repp. After a few minutes of prayer on the part of several people present, this motion was unanimously adopted, and Mr. Repp agreed that he would accept the responsibility if the A. R. A. found him satisfactory. In this same meeting the subscriptions in Portland were raised to more than $12,000.00.

Mr. Rickards was notified at once of the society's choice and upon being informed that Mr. Repp was an American citizen with no close relatives in Russia, a telegram arrived on August 31 with the welcome news: "Delighted to accept Repp. Have him report immediately in New York."

Before another week had gone by, letters began coming to Portland telling of branch organizations that were being formed in many parts of the United States, such as Montana and Washington; while other letters expressed an interest in the work and asked for further information.

Since the Volga Relief Society was very anxious for a maximum number of branches to begin functioning as quickly as possible, it was decided on September 4th that three Portland pastors were to visit communities in neighboring states and explain in greater detail the purposes and plans of the organization. One of these ministers, Rev. J. H. Hopp, left on the following day for Odessa, Washington, where an enthusiastic meeting was held on Tuesday, September 6th. The work there had already begun on August 30th when a branch society was organized and committees formed to canvas both the town and the surrounding rural territory. Rev. J. H. Eckhardt, who had been elected secretary-treasurer of the Odesso group, was to prove one of the most capable and loyal of all the ministers connected with relief operations.

After leaving Odessa, Rev. Hopp held meetings in Ritzville, Washington, where Rev. Jacob Morach and Mr. William Thiel headed the work. Then he went on to Dryden, where Rev. John Reister had already read Mr. Miller's circular letters to his congregation and had assisted in the raising of the first funds. The secretary of the organization, Mr. Ed Radach, should be mentioned as having been the first person in the United States to send his subscription list to Portland.

Rev. Hopp also met with the people of Alkalai Flats and of Endicott, Washington. Rev. C. J. Wagner assisted in the organization of a branch society in the latter town, and deserves a great deal of credit for the splendid work that was done there. The German-Russian people of Walla Walla, who chose Rev. Paul Krumbein as president, should also be commended for the great efficiency and generosity which they showed. It might be pointed out that all of these communities collected their money and sent it to Oregon with the most unusual speed; and in the case of three towns: Odessa, Walla Walla and Endicott, checks of $1836.81, $1400.00, and $1265.50 were forwarded less than three weeks after the receipt of their first report from Mr. Miller.

The second pastor, Rev. George Zocher, was sent to Fresno, California, where great concern over the German famine sufferers had been evident throughout the entire month of August. Upon the receipt of letters telling of the terrible conditions in Russia, many Fresno people sent their relatives packages of food or clothing through private concerns such as one called A. Fink and Sons. People from various colonies also formed relief committees designed to help their own specific village. Thus we hear of a Stahl Verein, a Dinkel, Straub, Warenburg, Kukkus, Verein, etc. Other individuals had turned to religious or charitable organizations such as the National Lutheran Council or the Red Cross, and had made inquiries regarding methods of relief.

In the midst of these discussions on ways and means of giving aid, the first message from Portland began to arrive, calling upon the people to form a united organization and to send their money to the Volga Relief Society for distribution by the A. R. A. In response to a letter from Rev. Albert Reiman of Dinuba, Mr. Miller wrote on August 29th:

> "From a California paper we notice that you were perhaps planning to do your work through a private concern, but investigation shows us that the small package business will not suffice in these trying times. It must be done on a larger scale, and that is why we have united with our government and intend to work through them."

Since Fresno, California with the neighboring towns of Sanger, Dinuba, Biola, etc., represents one of the most thickly populated areas in which Volga Germans have settled, the Portland organization was particularly anxious for a union with this state. Consequently, the following telegram dated September 4 was received with unusual satisfaction by Mr. Miller:

> "Following your letter of August 26, I wish to state that we had a mass meeting in the German Lutheran Cross Church today. A motion was made and carried by a large number that your Mr. George Repp shall be our representative for this work."

This telegram was signed by Mr. Andrew Wolf, the newly-elected president of the organization.

The enthusiasm with which the people of Fresno began their drive for funds is clearly shown in a second telegram sent on September 9 by Rev. W. J. Schmalle who announced:

> "Fresno has over $13,000.00 cash with good subscriptions already secured and canvassing going on enthusiastically. We hope to double the amount. California is pushing ahead. Look out for your laurels."

In the meantime Rev. George Zocher had arrived in

California and addressed a large mass meeting in Fresno on Sunday, September 18. He also visited the people living in Dinuba, Sanger and Barstow. With respect to the latter towns he wrote in a letter dated September 20:

> "The people of Dinuba have been unusually liberal in their contributions, although all of the churches have done fine work, and will do even more. The largest donation so far has been made by a man in Sanger who gave $1000.00 to the cause."

As a result of such remarkable generosity a check of $16,632.34, designated for eleven colonies such as Stahl, Warenburg, Straub, Dinkel, and Kukkus, was sent to Portland on September 19. Included in the sum was also $1796.34 for the General Fund.

Upon his return to Oregon, Rev. Zocher stopped at Lodi, California, where a relief society was formed under the leadership of Rev. G. L. Brakemeyer. Practically all of the German-speaking people in Lodi came from the Black Sea area of Russia, but in spite of this fact, they contributed $1544.15 to the unfortunate famine-sufferers of the Volga.

The third pastor, Rev. Henry Hagelganz, had been assigned the states of Nebraska, Colorado, and Montana. Upon leaving Portland he went directly to Lincoln from where a check of $190.77 had been sent to the Volga Relief Society on August 30. This money represented part of the funds that had been raised in one of the meetings that took place after August 7, when Rev. Suffa suggested that something be done to help the German people in Russia.

However, the real story of the Lincoln organization began when a physician, Dr. H. P. Wekesser, called a meeting of prominent Volga German business men to discuss the most practical way of actually forwarding money to Russia. At that time it was decided that Dr. Wekesser and Mr. J. J. Stroh were to go to Washington for a personal consultation with Herbert Hoover. The interview took place on August 30, and at Hoover's suggestion the men went on to New York where they met Mr. Edgar Rickard. To their great surprise they were informed by the A. R. A. officials that a society had already been organized in Portland, Oregon, and that consequently it would be desirable for the two bodies to co-ordinate their efforts in doing relief work among the German-Russian people of the United States.

Mr. Rickard then sent a wire to Portland suggesting that Mr. Repp stop in Nebraska while on his way to New York, and expressed the hope that it would be possible for one man to represent all Volga German communities. This telegram was received on September 1, but because of the limited time at Mr. Repp's disposal, it was thought that Rev. Hagelganz would be able to persuade the Nebraska communities to accept the suggestion of the A. R. A.

Nevertheless, the people of Lincoln felt that because of their central location, it would be more logical to have an independent organization to raise money in such states as Kansas, Nebraska, and Colorado. They also wished to maintain their own headquarters in the middle west, and asked for permission to send a second representative to Russia. As a result, a large mass meeting was held on September 9, and a separate organization called the Central States Volga Relief Society was formed. Two days later the following officers were chosen in the St. Paul's M. E. Church: Dr. H. P. Wekesser, president; M. J. J. Stroh, vice-president; Mr. John Lebsock, treasurer; and Mr. F. A. Lorenz, secretary.

An office was subsequently arranged for in the Orpheum Building, where Dr. Wekesser was located, and from here letters and reports were sent out to those towns in Kansas, Nebraska, Oklahoma, etc., that affiliated with the Lincoln group. During the following months the officers of the society, as well as other members such as Mr. H. J. Amen, Rev. Jacob Wagner, and Mr. Adolph Lebsock, visited many of these communities and performed a great service by arousing interest in the relief work done in Russia.

Finally on October 22 the A. R. A. agreed that a second representative could be sent to Russia "on condition that all money raised in the United States by the German-Russians should go into a joint fund to be distributed under their own direction." They also stipulated that both Mr. Repp and the Central States representative should be considered the agents of all relief societies organized by the German-Russian people in America. After consenting to these two provisions, the Lincoln organization unanimously chose Rev. Jacob Wagner as its representative in a mass meeting held on December 19. (4).

In accordance with the A. R. A. provision, all money sent by both the Central States Society and the Portland organization, as well as the sums forwarded directly to New York were credited to the Volga Relief Society. In future books published by the A. R. A. the total amount contributed is listed as $220,000.00 (5), but it should be pointed out that this figure includes the $70,000.00 that was so generously given by the Lincoln people, as well as what was raised by Portland.

After leaving Lincoln, Rev. Hagelganz conducted meetings at Hastings, McCook and Culbertson, Nebraska. The Volga Germans in all of these communities agreed to organize, and immediately began to raise funds for relief purposes. The people of Hastings later voted to forward their money to the A. R. A. through the Lincoln society, but the two other communities sent theirs to Portland. In all of these towns Rev. Hagelganz found his audience both willing and eager to help. In fact the larger part of the $2521.30 sent by Culbertson and the $3062.80 sent by McCook was subscribed within a few weeks' time. Much of the credit for the success of these organizations should go to the capable officers in charge, such as J. J. Klein, the president of the McCook branch, and Rev. John H. Strohecker, the president at Culbertson.

From Nebraska Rev. Hagelganz went on to Colorado where he held meetings in such towns as Fort Collins, Fort Morgan and Denver. In the later city an additional $300.00 was contributed to the fund in order to persuade the Portland pastor to sing a song in the Russian language. The interest which Rev. Hagelganz was able to arouse in the people of Colorado helped to make these branches some of the most active in the entire United States.

It would be impossible to mention all the people who

assisted in the work which was so enthusiastically begun, but Rev. Elias Hergert of Fort Collins, Rev. H. G. Zorn of Brush, Mr. H. P. Weber of Fort Morgan, and Mr. David Kisler of Denver should all be commended for the efficient way in which they headed their societies. The people of Sterling, where Rev. O. K. Henzel and Rev. F. W. Schlitzkus were stationed, also organized with the neighboring town of Atwood, which was represented by Rev. F. Bunge and Mr. G. Jacob Fritzler. As a result of the outstanding leadership of these four men and the wonderful spirit of the people, $3000 was raised less than thirty days after the work was begun.

Credits should also be given to Rev. John Hoelzer, a traveling missionary for the German Congregational churches, who was living in Denver at the time. Rev. Hoelzer was personally acquainted with the Portland officials and in his travels among the Volga German people performed a great service by instilling confidence in the Volga Relief Society.

The third state on Rev. Hagelganz's itinerary was Montana. The two cities of Billings and Laurel had organized a branch society as early as August 30, and at the very first meeting had raised $1300.00 Upon his arrival in Billings, Rev. Hagelganz was driven by Rev. Fred Anhorn to Laurel, where the people had been told that a church bell would announce his arrival. The eagerness with which they were waiting for more detailed news from Portland is shown by the fact that in just a few minutes' time the entire church was filled. As a result of this and subsequent meetings, the Volga-Germans of Billings and Laurel raised a total sum of $3965.35 for their friends and relatives in Russia.

In the meantime letters responding to Mr. Miller's first circulars continued to arrive in Portland. The German-Russians in the Canadian Cities of Calgary, Leader, Trochu, and Winnipeg, all sent checks consisting of more than $500.00. The people living in Ramona, Kansas formed a society under the capable leadership of Mr. Conrad Kleiber and Mr. John Schnell, and eventually sent $1370.00 to the western organization. In Weatherford, Oklahoma, the branch was headed by

Rev. J. P. Kaiser, who was able to accomplish splendid results in a community with so few people. In Flint, Michigan, Mr. Jacob Aab and Mr. Philip Gross succeeded in raising $1186.00; and in Pine Island, New York similarly generous results were obtained by the branch president, Mr. Edward Weiss.

Probably the greatest surprise that the Portland officials ever had was when a check of $243.76 arrived from San Antonia, Argentina. No correspondence had ever been sent to South America, and it can only be surmised that people living in the United States wrote to relatives in that country telling them of the work of the Volga Relief Society and advising them to send their money to Portland.

Other states from which money was sent were the two Dakotas, Idaho, Wyoming, Iowa, Wisconsin, Illinois, and Minnesota; so that before the year was over funds had been received from one hundred and one towns of the United States, Canada and South America. A complete list of all these communities with the money raised in each place will be included in a later chapter.

During the first week of September, while the task of organizing these branches went on, there was also a great deal of activity in Portland. Mrs. Repp had planned to go to Russia with her husband, but on September 6th a telegram arrived from New York saying, "We are sending no women into Russia. Impossible for Mrs. Repp to accompany husband further than England or Germany." She then decided very wisely that she could do much more good by staying in Portland and assisting in the Relief work there. This was evidently also the opinion of the society because on that very evening she was elected to succeed her husband as secretary, and he was given the new position of general secretary and representative in Russia.

On the night of September 7th an impressive farewell banquet was given Mr. Repp in the Ebenezer Congregational Church, and an additional $12,630.00 was pledged for the famine sufferers. This increased the Portland people's contributions to $31,630.00, all of which had been subscribed in less than one month. (6).

Two days later Mr. Repp left for New York. He arrived on September 13 and reported immediately to Mr. Rickard, who told him that arrangements had been made for his passage on September 17 aboard the steamship "Kroonland." Before leaving for Europe he also had interviews with Mr. Frank Page, assistant secretary of the A. R. A. and Mr. Herbert Hoover, who headed the organization. Both of these men were very much interested in the history of the Volga Germans, and in Mr. Repp's plans for carrying on relief work among them. All interviews were evidently completely satisfactory because on the following day a telegram arrived in Portland saying, "Mr. Hoover met Repp yesterday and approves your selection. Asks us express congratulations success your organization. Repp sails Saturday."

In reading about the organization of the Volga Relief Society one cannot help but notice the remarkable speed with which all these events took place. It is difficult to realize that the first meeting of the society was held on August 11; that the first money was raised on August 18, which was two days before an agreement had even been made by the A. R. A. with Soviet Russia; that a representative was chosen on August 25, and on September 17 he was already sailing for Russia. Then on September 22, less than one month after the sending of the first circular letter, Mr. Gottfried Geist was able to announce that the Volga Relief Society had placed $40,433.24 on deposit for the A.R.A., and Mrs. George Repp added that $73,552.68 had been subscribed by the members of the Portland and the branch societies.

FOOTNOTES

1. Unless otherwise indicated, all quotations in this and subsequent chapters are taken from the files of the Volga Relief Society in the possession of Mr. and Mrs. George Repp.
2. **"Literary Digest"**, August 13, 1921.
3. H. H. Fisher, **op. cit.**, 52-53.
4. G. F. Schmidt, **"Bericht der American Volga Relief Society"**, 4.
5. H. H. Fisher, **op. cit.**, 467.
6. The amount of money eventually paid by the people of Portland was $29,576.86. This discrepancy arises from the fact that some of the pledges were later changed to Food Drafts which could be sent to specific individuals.

Chapter Three.

FEEDING BEGINS IN THE FAMINE AREA.

Immediately after leaving New York on the "Kroonland", Mr. Repp met ex-governor Goodrich of Indiana who was being sent to Russia as a personal representative of Herbert Hoover, with the task of reporting back to him after having made a survey of conditions there. During the eleven days that it took to cross the Atlantic, the two men had many opportunities to discuss the Russian situation, and Governor Goodrich developed a keen interest in the Volga Germans which was to be of great importance later on.

Upon arriving in London, they visited the European A. R. A. chief, Walter Lyman Brown, who had made the agreement with Litvinov on August 2. After a short conversation, Mr. Repp was asked if he cared to sign a contract which would make him a regular member of the A. R. A. staff. This suggestion was naturally accepted, although it came as a great surprise, since it had been understood in Portland that the Volga Relief representative would work only in co-operation with the organization, and not as one of its regular men. As a result of this change in the A. R. A. policy —which must be interpreted as a great compliment to the impression Repp had made — he was now given a daily expense account, which made it unnecessary for his own society to send him any funds as long as he remained in Russia.

Two days after their arrival in London, Goodrich and Repp left for the continent. Their route took them from Dover to Ostend and then across Germany to Riga, Latvia which at that time was the port of entry taken by practically all visitors of the Soviet Union. On October 4th the train crossed the border at Sebesh, and immediately the Americans were introduced to two typical Russian characteristics: delay and bribery. The customs inspection lasted so long that Mr. Repp had an opportunity to take a long walk to a near-by hill. Upon returning to the train he was asked by Gov. Goodrich to make sure that their luggage had been put on board, but upon investigating, he was told that the baggage car contained no available room for their suitcases. However, the transfer of a few rubles suddenly changed the whole situation and in a few minutes time, sufficient space was miraculously found!

On the following day, the train moved slowly through eastern Russia. Along the way crawling freight trains were seen closely packed with gaunt Baltic refugees who had been prisoners of war in Soviet Russia and were now returning to their own countries. The men also noticed that the further east they went the more dilapidated the buildings became, and the more poverty-stricken the people appeared. Upon their arrival in Moscow the city itself gave an impression of desolation and despair that easily disheartened the most optimistic newcomer. In the words of Mr. Golder, one of the A. R. A. men:

> "The destructive effects of the war and the revolution are all about. The railway sidings are crowded with worn-out locomotives and broken-down cars, the railway yards are prowling places for starving men and hungry dogs, and the railway station is in neglect and confusion, full of sickly, ragged, and famishing refugees with the look of despair and death on their faces. On the streets are heaps of refuse, the accumulation of two or three years; and off the streets are tumble-down houses, the door and woodwork having been turned into fuel and the lower floors into public toilets. There were few vehicles about, and these kicked up clouds of dust as they zigzagged along to escape the ruts and holes. We drove two or three miles through the city, from the station to our headquarters, and I do not recall seeing a half-dozen open shops. There were comparatively few people on the street, and they looked ragged and lifeless." (1).

Walter Duranty, who was one of the first American correspondents to reach Moscow, also describes the city in his book "I Write As I Please." According to him there had been no running water or steam heat in Moscow for two and one-half years. As a result,—

> "People built themselves little stoves of brick in each room . . . and burnt what they could, beams and framework from broken houses, green wood from the parks and

woods around the city, their own furniture and last their floors and doors. . . . When a window got broken they nailed a board across because there was no more glass. Later they took the board for fuel and sealed up the window with clay and bricks . . . I've talked a great deal to people in Moscow about the 'bad years', and all of them say that the worst thing was not hunger or cold, though both were bad enough, but the breakdown of the water supply and sanitation . . . . In a big modern building the effects of this break-down must have been appalling." (2).

Duranty also mentions the closed shops that had impressed Mr. Golder, and tells that in a six-mile walk through the streets of Moscow, he saw no open establishments except beauty parlors, shops selling scientific apparatus, and a few dingy stores with cabbages, potatoes and wizened pears and apples. The clothes of the people also presented a strange appearance since many of them had been sewn together from blankets, curtains or carpets, and one little girl was even seen wearing a valuable Persian prayer rug. In practically all cases the people were dirty and their clothes were dirty because there was no soap with which to wash them.

The A. R. A. had opened its first kitchens in Petrograd on September 7th and in Moscow four days later. Since practically all of the children asked to be fed, it was necessary to choose only the most seriously undernourished, which represented about forty per cent of the entire number. While this was being done, an investigating committee was sent to the cities of Kazan, Simbirsk, and Samara on the Volga, so that when Mr. Repp arrived in Moscow, preparations for child-feeding had already been begun in those places. However, there had not been sufficient time to enable the men to open any kitchens in the German villages which lay south of Saratov.

A description of the horrible suffering in the Volga towns visited by this first A. R. A. contingent is given by Walter Duranty who states:

"The first thing I saw and smelled was a refugee camp of about fifteen thousand peasants in a big open space outside the railroad station at Samara. . . These poor wretches had floated in from surrounding villages when they knew beyond doubt that the crops had failed, when their own meagre stock of food was exhausted and they knew that to stay where they were meant swift and certain death. The adults were wane and haggard but far less dreadful than the children, who looked like spiders with fat bloated bellies and thin shriveled limbs. That came from eating clay and bark and refuse, which they were unable to digest. . . . They sat there in their dust and squalor waiting for death, without food or shelter and the only movement among them was the steady train of stretcher-bearers carrying off the dead to burial." (3).

We also have the following paragraph from a pamphlet written by Anna J. Haines, a Quaker Representative in Russia:

"I could hear the children crying two blocks away as I approached one of the homes for abandoned children in Samara, the central city of the famine area of Russia. A steady wail that kept up like a moan grew louder as we got nearer. The nurses could do nothing except to go around every morning and separate the babies that were going to die that day; and they went around at different times later and felt them to see if they were cold. In the evening those who had died during the day were gathered together and placed in heaps outside the building. A garbage cart stopped each night and the baby bodies were loaded in. The garbage carts stopped in the same way before all of the children's institutions in Samara and the other cities in the Volga region." (4).

After hearing such stories of conditions in the famine area, Mr. Repp was naturally very anxious to reach the German colonies as soon as possible. As a result, he stayed only long enough to receive necessary instructions, and then took a train for Samara on October 10. On this trip he was accompanied by an interpreter who had formerly been a political prisoner but had been set free by the communists. The man evidently took his duties very seriously, because during the night he kept a gun beside him and at the slightest noise would jump to his feet ready to attack any possible intruder. Such solicitude seemed a trifle overdone in Mr. Repp's opinion, and as a result, he decided to continue his journey alone.

At Samara a conference was held with Governor Goodrich and two A. R. A. men, Mr. Golder and Mr. Hutchinson, who had left Moscow an a previous train. It was agreed that they were to move southward by rail, going through Penza on the way, while Repp was to leave for Saratov on a Volga steamer. A boat was expected that very evening, but it failed to arrive until five o'clock the next morning. As a result, Mr. Repp spent a very uncomfortable night at the harbor, since nobody had any definite information regarding the delay. When the steamer finally did dock, it was necessary for him to battle his way through an immense crowd of peasants, all of whom were trying to get on board. While this was going on, the captain wrung his hands and protested that there was no more available room, although eventually a cabin was found for both Repp and a Russian lawyer whom he had introduced as his interpreter.

After staying in Samara all day the steamboat left at seven o'clock that night. It seemed to move unbearably slow, according to its impatient American passenger, but finally on the morning of October 14 the city of Saratov was reached. The description of the scene that confronted the passengers as they approached the shore can best be given in Mr. Repp's own words:

> "The first thing we saw was from fifteen hundred to two thousand people on the banks of the Volga, without food and in rags, mostly Germans, and all bound for somewhere, none of them knowing really where they wanted to go, but just to get away. Everything they possessed in this world they had with them; a good many were sick from exposure and hunger. They went about the city of Saratov picking up potato peelings, melon rinds, cabbage leaves, and in fact, anything that could be eaten. As fast as they could get transportation, either north, south, east, or west, by rail or boat, they left. Those Germans that did not get transportation were in a way taken care of by Pastor Seib's church."

After a one-day survey of the city, the following letter, dated October 15, was sent to the Volga Relief Society:

> "The German people of Saratov that always make this their home are not suffering from want, since food can be bought, such as black and white bread, vegetables, meat, etc., and also shoes. The prices are very high, although salaries are sufficient for staple articles, but not luxuries such as sugar, white bread, etc.
>
> "I made a trip to a German refugee home. People in this home wandered in from the colonies because all their food had been consumed. Naturally nothing but starvation stared them in the face. They came mostly from the east

side of the Volga known as "Wiesenseite." A good many are sick and some very very thin, and all terribly dirty. They have no ambition to clean up around the building or their rooms. In fact, they are at a stage that I cannot describe.

"On the bank of the Volga River in Saratov, I found a group of Germans all bound for the United States or Canada. After I informed them it was impossible to get there, their hearts fell. After a long discussion, they decided to try to get into Germany. All have friends in America but not of our people in Portland.

"Walking about I saw a woman that looked German so I stepped up to her and said, 'Why so sad?' She told me her story. She, with her husband had lived for five happy years in a small colony. He was a blacksmith, and earned enough money for a comfortable living. When they saw that nothing but starvation stared them in the face they came on to Saratov two months ago. Meanwhile two of their children have starved. Two weeks ago her mother who had been living with them left. Her husband escorted her to the depot and never returned. Since then her other baby has died. She had no money so the government buried the baby. They laid it out very nicely but when they got to the cemetery it was thrown into a grave without a casket or anything to cover the little body—only the earth.

"From what I can learn, conditions are worse in the colonies. Today, after making a trip through the worst district I wept. Men, women, and children are continually begging for bread along the streets, but you know I cannot take care of them all. I have seen conditions where suicide in my opinion is not sin. I realize this is a horrible statement, but if I could find words to describe the horror of it all, you could not believe me. As a layman of relief work, I see only one salvation for thousands and that is premature death. I realize that noble work is being done in the United States and Canada but the field is large. The people are different from what you imagine. they do not weep. I cannot remember seeing a tear. Their sufferings are beyond that stage and the other people here that are better off gradually become accustomed to conditions."

On Sunday, October 16, Mr. Repp attended service in the beautiful Lutheran church of Saratov. He wrote that approximately one hundred people were present: that they were well dressed, clean and warm, and showed no signs of hunger.

Two days later, the A. R. A. men left on various survey trips. Goodrich and Repp, in whom we are most interested, decided to visit Marxstadt, the capital of the newly-formed German Republic on the Volga. From here they went to five or six German villages on the Wiesenseite of the river, where famine conditions were found to be unusually bad. In Marxstadt itself they found that there were about seven children's homes for orphans, and that each home had from fifty to seventy-five children. The homes were clean but could provide very little food and clothing.

The return trip across the river to Saratov was made in the same boat with Mr. Golder, who has the following story to tell:

"October 21, 1921—Hutchinson and I finished our investigations by one o'clock and were ready to leave for Saratov by two, but our departure was delayed as usual. Our passenger list had been considerably increased by Governor Goodrich and Repp (who had reached Marxstadt the night before), with their staff of three men, and by Russian officials of one kind and another. Our two small cabins were crowded, but we did not mind because we expected to reach Saratov in about three hours. Within twelve miles of our destination we ran into a fog, and the captain refused to move. Our native Volga guests or hosts—it was hard to know what their status was—settled themselves down into comfortable corners and fell asleep. The Governor, Hutchison, and I, played poker, with a place to sleep as stakes. The Governor got an empty corner, Hutchinson the top of a table, and I that part of the lounge that was not occupied. It was very hot in the cabin, but some of our visitor-hosts kept on their overcoats and closed the port holes whenever we were not looking. Some time during the night the fog lifted and we steamed into port." (5).

One of the guest-hosts who had caused Frank Golder so much discomfort during the night was Mr. Suppes, the Soviet Commissar for the German colonies. However, his actions can be explained by the fact that he had tuberculosis at the time and was actually a very sick man. Mr. Suppes was an unusually honest person, and had joined the Communist party with the most sincere motives. He soon became a very good friend of Mr. Repp, and although neither was ever convinced of the fallacy of his own political beliefs, they learned to respect each other's ability and honesty. Suppes was once described as the most stupid official in Russia, because all the other communists were using their position in order to amass a large fortune, but he himself remained as poor as ever.

After returning to Saratov from Marxstadt, both Repp and Governor Goodrich were very anxious to visit the "Berg" or west side of the river. This was accomplished by traveling on a boat as far south as Schilling, and from there to Balzar, Kutter, Alt Dönnhof, and Norka where Mr. Repp himself was born.

One of the things that the men noticed upon their arrival in a village was the unusual quiet that existed. The ordinary sounds of shouting children, barking dogs, or moving wagons were all gone, and the only signs of life that still remained were the people who could be seen moving listlessly around. A very large number of houses were also standing empty, because the occupants had either been killed in the Civil War or had left the village in the hope of finding food somewhere else.

Since there was no fodder on hand for the horses and livestock, it had become customary to remove the thatch from the roofs of these empty houses, knock out the dust, and then give it to the animals for food. This thatch had often been in use for as many as eight or ten years, and consequently the Americans were not surprised to notice that the horses and cattle were invariably skinny and under-nourished.

Mr. Repp and Governor Goodrich always made it a point to drive directly to the administrative headquarters of the village, where routine questions were asked on the number of deaths in the current year, the amount of food still on hand and the necessity for American aid. They found that in every case starvation had already come to some of the poorest inhabitants of the community. People were at a point where everybody was for himself. Very few had any food to spare, and even when an owner still had some animals out on the fields, he was afraid to give anything away, because the thought would always come that he might need it for himself before very long.

According to a letter written by Mr. Repp. "it was very evident that 75% of the inhabitants would die before the 1922 harvest unless help came from the outside world. We found them at this time eating horses, camels, dogs, cats, field mice, bark of trees and some people that had a little rye flour left would mix this with earth and eat it."

After the two men returned to Saratov and gave their report on conditions in the villages, the A. R. A. office decided that the region inhabited by the Volga German colonists was too large for one man to handle. Consequently, Paul Clapp, one of their workers, was assigned to the east side of the river, while Repp was given the west side. Plans for the opening of kitchens were immediately made, and on October 28 all available food that was on hand in Saratov was loaded on two ships and started down the Volga. Mr. Repp went with one to Schilling and Mr. Clapp with the other to Seelmann. The Bergseite ship alone carried 538 pood of sugar, 681 pood beans, 3432 pood flour, 20 cases cocoa with 240 pounds to the case, 800 cases of milk, 25 barrels of fat, with 50 gallons per barrel, and 1177 pood rice. (6).

In a letter written to his wife Mr. Repp described this as one of the happiest days of his life. It is also easy to imagine the joy with which these two boats were greeted by the people in Schilling and Seelmann, and how gladly the inhabitants helped with the work of unloading. During the previous months the Soviet government had often made promises of aid, that had remained unfulfilled, but the people now realized that it was possible to rely with more confidence on the word of the Americans.

However, before the kitchens could be opened, it was necessary that arrangements be made for the transportation of the food to the inland villages as well as for the preparation of the cooked meals. The first of these tasks was accomplished by enlisting the help of the men who still had horses and wagons with which they could drive to the river towns and bring back the cases of supplies. Since only the poorest children were at first fed, there was sometimes a little difficulty in persuading the wealthier members of the village to assist in this task, but as a whole they were glad to be

of service, even when their own families failed to benefit thereby.

The second task involved the making of arrangements for the actual feeding of the children. This
was done by means of a committee that was appointed
in each village to take charge of the kitchen. If we refer again to Mr. Repp's report we are told that:

"The committee usually consisted of the 'Vorsteher',
Secretary, Pastor, Doctor, if there was one, and three or
four members of the church board, depending upon the
size of the village. The duties of the committee were first
to provide a place to cook, a place to eat, to supply the
wood and water, and to be responsible for the supplies
until they were actually consumed. The committee also
selected the cooks and those children who were to eat in
the kitchens. It was my duty to select this committee in
the Bergseite villages, and Mr. Clapp's duty to select the
committee in his territory; in fact, the American that was
in charge always kept control over the distribution of the
American food. Needless to say, there were always a few
in a colony that criticized and hampered the work of the
committee, usually for some selfish reason; and occasionally charges were brought against the committee by those
few that were dissatisfied, but every charge that was open-
ly brought against them and investigated was found false."

As a result of their years of experience in relief
work, the A. R.A. had developed three broad principles
which were carried out by Mr. Repp as well as all the
other Americans in Russia. These were: First, relief
to those who needed it most without regard to race, religion or politics. Second, the food had to be eaten by
the children at the feeding post where it was prepared
under A. R. A. direction. Third, strict accounting for all
food and funds in order to prevent waste or misuse. In
order to carry out this last principle armed guards were
always stationed before all the warehouses in the harbor towns and also in the villages of the interior. (7).

The first kitchen on the Bergseite was supposed to
open in Schilling on November 2, but it took a little additional time for the work of organization to get completed. About 200 children of the village were chosen
from the poorest families and naturally they felt a
great deal of impatience at the delay. Mr. Repp tells the
story of a little boy who asked him wistfully, "Uncle,
when WILL the kitchens open?", and upon being told

that the cooks were a little slow, he suggested an immediate remedy, "Let's throw them in the Volga"!

We do not have an account describing the happy day in Schilling when the children were fed for the first time, but on November 10 Rev. F. Wacker, the pastor of the German church in Norka wrote a long letter to Mrs. Repp telling what had occurred in his village. He mentions that on November 7th Mr. Repp reached Norka and organized a committee of thirteen men who were put in charge of the arrangements for the feeding. It was decided that kitchens were to be opened in the two school houses of the village and in the summer kitchen of the schoolteacher. In the meantime, the Soviet officials saw to it that all necessary wood, water, and utensils were on hand for the actual cooking. As had been arranged, the food itself was brought in wagons from Schilling, and in three days time enough had arrived to last for six weeks.

The most difficult task of the committee, according to Rev. Wacker, was to pick out the children who were to receive their daily meal from the A.R.A. There were over two thousand youngsters in Norka, but only 500 of them could be fed on opening day. The committee found it necessary to visit every home, and to investigate personally the need of each family. There was naturally a great deal of disappointment and unhappiness in those families whose children were not selected. Rev. Wacker was even interrupted in his letter writing by a twelve-year-old boy who burst into tears when he was told that he alone could eat in the kitchen, but that his brother and sister would have to stay at home.

Another difficult problem was to pick out the women who were to do the cooking. Although they were to receive no pay except a double portion of food, a throng of candidates besieged the committee. One woman was so anxious to know if her application would be accepted, that she even went to a fortune-teller for the answer; and another became quite ill in her excitement. But finally this question was also settled "with tears of joy for those who were chosen, and tears of sorrow for those who had been dropped."

In a latter letter Rev. Wacker tells the story of the opening day: (8).

> "On the morning of November 14th the smoke from the kitchen chimneys rose to the wintry heavens. Every child who possessed an admittance card armed himself with a plate and a spoon. Although the food was not to be served until noon, the kitchens reminded one of a besieged fortress at ten o'clock already . . . Finally the doors opened, and in wild confusion the horde rushed in. The members of the committee had a difficult time bringing order out of the confusion, but finally every child found a place . . . A board which had been placed over two school benches acted as a serving table. Upon it lay pieces of bread which blinded one with their whiteness. None of us had seen such bread for years, and to the poorer children it was something entirely new. From here I went into the kitchen where two cooks were stirring the rice porridge, which was being cooked in ten or twelve large kettles. This was Monday and according to the American program, cocoa should have been prepared, but because of the bad roads from Schilling, it had not arrived as yet. Consequently, the children were given rice porridge on two successive days. In the meantime, the members of the committee were showing the children to their places.. . . Everything seemed to be taking too long in the little fellows' opinion, and as some waited for their names to be read, the others, who already had a place moved impatiently on their benches in expectation of the things that were to come. Several of them examined their plates once more on the outside and inside, as if they wanted to convince themselves that none of the precious porridge would be lost."

At this point Rev. Wacker left the first kitchen in order to visit the other two. By the time he reached them, the children were already eating and everything was progressing satisfactorily. He tells about one tiny youngster who was sitting at a bench that was much too high for him, so that his little nose was level with his plate. In order to remedy this situation he finally set the plate on his lap, holding it with one hand, and his spoon with the other. However, this meant that there was no free hand for his bread, so he returned the plate to the bench and tried to eat in a standing position. Finally his mother came to his rescue, and the problem was solved by his being held on her lap, and continuing his meal "with an expression of great contentment."

Another child whom Rev. Wacker noticed was a little three-year-old girl who seemed to be afraid to take some of the bread when it was carried around in a large basket. He says, "I do not know if it was mere shyness or if she suddenly could not understand the meaning of it all. She had always heard that strange men would come and take away the people's bread, but now strange men had come and brought bread; not out of clay or of mixed barley and watermelon rind, but instead of beautiful clean flour."

The description of what occurred in Norka may be used as an example for all the German-speaking villages along the Volga. Both Mr. Clapp and Mr. Repp worked with the utmost speed, so that on December 2nd the latter was able to report that he was then feeding 9085 children in 24 villages. He had also made arrangements to open up kitchens in the remaining 59 German colonies on the Bergseite, and wrote that before very long, 30,000 children would be fed.

In the meantime Mr. Clapp had reported that he was feeding 8,085 children on November 30th, and also hoped to expand in the very near future. A more detailed account of the conditions that he had found on the Wiesenseite will be given in the next chapter.

FOOTNOTES
1. Golder and Hutchinson, **op. cit.,** 27-28.
2. Walter Duranty, **"I Write as I Please",** 110-112.
3. **Ibid,** 128.
4. American Friends Service Committee, **Bulletin No. 45.**
5. Golder and Hutchinson, **op. cit.,** 88-89.
6. A pood equals 36 American pounds, and 40 Russian pounds.
7. H. H. Fisher, **op. cit.,** 102-103.
8. All letters from Volga Germans in Russia were written in the German language and have been translated by the author. The quotations are sometimes given in a more condensed version, but the original meaning is intact.

Chapter Four.

THE EXPANSION OF CHILD-FEEDING IN RUSSIA.

When Mr. Hoover sent his first cablegram to Russia answering Maxim Gorki's plea for help, he made the statement that the A. R. A. was prepared to feed one million children. The speed and efficiency with which this promise was carried out is shown by the fact that although the first kitchen did not open until September 7, 1921, Mr. Page was able to report that on January 1, 1922, 1,025,000 boys and girls up to the age of fifteen were receiving a daily meal from the A. R. A.

However, the American workers soon realized that the situation was actually far more serious than they had expected, and as a result, more and more children's names were added to the relief rolls. The highest peak was eventually reached in August, 1922, when 4,174,339 youngsters were receiving food at the kitchens. (1).

This constant increase in aid was also felt among the German colonists. We have already heard that the first kitchen on the Bergseite was opened in Schilling on Novemeber 6th, and that in a very short time children were being fed in twenty-four neighboring villages such as Beideck, Balzer, Kutter, Huck, Norka, Dönnhof, Moor, Messer, Grimm, etc. All of these communities were close enough to Schilling that wagons could be sent to bring back the necessary supplies. One month later sufficient food was on hand so that Mr. Repp was able to increase the number of children being fed in these villages from 9085 to approximately 15,000. But since it was now the middle of December, the Volga River was a solid sheet of ice, and it was impossible for any boats to leave the harbors with supplies. As a result, the local committees in each village were notified to send sleighs and sledges to the A. R. A. warehouse at Pokrowsky, which lies across the river from Saratov. This practice was continued during the following winter months, until the Volga was again open for traffic after the spring thaws.

PEOPLE CALLING FOR AMERICAN FOOD FOR KITCHEN MEDWEDZ.

A more difficult problem was presented by such colonies as Frank, Walter, Hussenbach, Köhler, etc., which lie so far east of the river that they could not take advantage of the first shipment of food to Schilling. Consequently, it was necessary for their supplies to be sent by rail to the Medwediza station from which they were transported by wagons or sleighs to the neighboring towns. Mr. Repp was soon to discover that although the distance from Saratov to Medwediza was very small, the Russian railroads were in such a deplorable condition that it actually took several weeks for the food to reach its destination. Because of this unavoidable delay the people of Frank and other communities of this area were not able to open their kitchens until the end of December.

At the same time that relief operations began in the eastern villages, similar arrangements were made in the colonies lying south of Schilling, such as Dobrinka, Schwab, Holstein, Galka, etc., so that by January 1, 1922, thirty-five additional colonies with approximately 15,000 children were being taken care of.

This means that a total number of 30,000 children in 59 villages of the Bergseite were receiving a daily meal at the beginning of the new year.

At no time was the feeding of the children carried on entirely according to the population of the village, since the condition of some colonies was much worse than that of others. For example, on December 14, 1000 children were being fed in Norka, 1200 in Messer, 1700 in Grimm, and 1250 in Moor. Mr. Repp wrote in explanation of these figures:

> "You will note that although Norka is the largest colony, Messer, Grimm and Moor have larger kitchens. These colonies have much less food, and are in very bad shape. The village of Grimm, which had a population of 6,200 in November, lost 1000 people this year. Messer, with a population of 3772 in November, had 717 deaths during the year; while Moor with a population of 3800 had 638 deaths. Many of these dead bodies lie unburied in the cemeteries because the people say that they have not the strength to dig a grave."

Because of this variation in poverty, some of the villages were soon being given enough food for all of their children, whereas, in other places, only one-half or two-thirds of the youngsters were fed.

In the meantime the poorest children in the German villages of the Wiesenseite were also being given a daily meal by the A. R. A. A great deal of the credit for this initial work should go to Mr. Paul Clapp, who opened up most of the kitchens on the east side of the river, although a small group of German colonies north of Marxstadt was placed under the jurisdiction of Mr. Russell Cobb. Later in the winter, Mr. Gustave Beschorner, a representative of the National Lutheran Council, was stationed at Krasni Kut, which lies on a railroad going east from Marxstadt. In addition, Mr. Repp made several trips through the colonies, and kept in constant touch with the progress of the work.

All of the men on the Wiesenseite had a great deal to contend with as far as the Soviet Commissars are concerned. One of these officials was a notorious woman called "Frau Fuchs" who had served in the Communist Women's Legion of Death. She was always seen carrying a six-shooter, and because of her great political power, was able to hold the German people in her district in abject terror. By taking advantage of their fear, she often forced the colonists to sell her the contents of the $10.00 Food Draft packages, which were later introduced, in exchange for whatever she was willing to give them. This was a very serious crime according to Soviet law, but nobody had the courage to report her. Finally one of the A. R. A. men found a bag of American goods in her possession, and this frightened her so much that in the future her reign of intimidation and terrorization was greatly moderated.

In one of Mr. Clapp's reports dated November 30, he told of his first meeting with the Soviet officials in Seelmann. He informed them that the A. R. A. was prepared to feed 10,000 children within a radius of fifty versts, and asked for a list of the villages in this area with the number of children in each community. That same afternoon a warehouse was chosen for the storage of the A. R. A. food which Mr. Clapp had brought on a steamer with him. The head of the local Soviet supplied a company of soldiers to unload the boat and to guard the goods during the night.

With the help of these officials, Mr. Clapp was given the names of 58 villages which had an estimated population of 31,000 children from one to fourteen years of age. It was decided that at least twelve northern villages were to get their supplies from the railroad station at Krasni Kut, but the larger number, including such places as Straub, Warenburg, Dinkel, etc., were to come to Seelmann. The report then continues:

"As soon as the food had been placed in the warehouse at Seelmann, the Local Committee immediately advised the German villages in the district either by telegram or courier, to come for food. The condition of the horses is such that from three to five days are required for travel from the outlying districts to Seelmann.

"As soon as the food had left Seelmann for the fifteen villages extending northward to Probander, I traveled from village to village organizing the local committees and opened kitchens. . . . The food is stored in each instance in a suitable warehouse and is under constant guard. . . . The committees and kitchen managers are instructed in the general rules for child feeding as laid down by the Saratov headquarters. Each child has a card, and a weekly report is made by each kitchen manager showing the number of children fed daily and the quantity of food disbursed and on hand. . . . Many of the kitchens are in the schoolhouses, since there is no school due to the shortage of wood.

"The reports of starvation have not been exaggerated. Only a small percentage of the population now have bread. I, personally, visited two or three families in each of the fifteen villages, and inspected many of the children. The children were badly swollen from starvation. They are starving day by day and the situation is steadily growing worse. Horses are being killed for food, and it is only a matter of time until there will be practically no livestock left. As far as I can determine, the only relief which has been administered by the Soviet government in the Seelmann district was a delivery of approximately two hundred and fifty poods of potatoes to each village. This amounted to less than one pood of potatoes to each family, practically nothing. I was told in a number of the villages that within the past three weeks a levy had been made on them by the government for foodstuffs which had to be delivered to Seelmann and Kukkus. . . .

"Naturally, the general population cannot understand why they are called upon to make these deliveries of foodstuffs from their last available supplies, when they themselves are in the face of absolute starvation.

"The situation looks almost desperate and although we may be able to save the lives of a great many children by our feeding, it is impossible to predict what will happen to the general adult population.

"As winter comes on it will be increasingly difficult for a considerable number of the children in each village to come into the kitchens on account of the lack of clothing and shoes. I have personally investigated this situation and find it is absolutely true. . . . This fact is further substantiated by the absence at kitchens of children holding cards, on cold days. Any relief that you can give in the way of old clothing, or of clothing and shoes for children is most urgently needed." (2).

In spite of the discouraging conditions that both Mr. Clapp and Mr. Repp found, one must not forget the happiness of the Volga Germans in hearing that from now on their children would receive a daily meal of American food. Their gratitude is shown by the fact that throughout the entire winter and spring of 1921-1922 hundreds of letters were sent to Portland expressing the thankfulness of the people for the help which was given by the A. R. A. One of these accounts came from Rev. Streck, the pastor of the church in Grimm, who told of Mr. Repp's first visit to this village:

"Already in September we heard a message that resounded in our ears as a welcome song out of a distant beautiful land, 'Help is coming from America'. How we waited then, day and night; for our need was truly great, and was constantly increasing. Even officially Grimm is recognized as one of the poorest villages in this district. But when nothing happened, the doubters began to announce 'There's nothing to it again except empty idle talk.' It was very difficult for me to encourage the people of the community with the words, 'Just a little more patience; help will surely come'. And finally it came!

"On the fifteenth of November as I sat in my study thinking unhappily of all the distress and suffering around me, a guest was announced. He entered with the words, 'My name is Repp, and I come from America'. In my joy I felt like answering 'Blessed be the day of thy coming, brother from afar'. Without wasting any time, we organized a committee of six members to make the necessary arrangements for the opening of three kitchens in which 800 of the poorest children were to be fed. It was very late at night before our guest could go to bed. He had come a great distance that day, over exceedingly bad roads and on a dilapidated-looking wagon. But early the next morning he left for the neighboring village of Franzosen to continue his work there." (3).

One of the things that often touched Mr. Repp very much was the generosity of the children in wanting to share what they received in the kitchens with their more unfortunate brothers and sisters. An incident of this kind is described in a letter written by Konrad Würtz of Beideck on November 7, 1921:

> "The people of Beideck are grateful to all of you that 360 children are now being fed in our village. George Repp, who brought the necessary supplies for the kitchen, asked me to go along with him for an inspection visit. We noticed a five-year-old child which had divided its bread. Repp asked, 'Child, why don't you eat all of your food'?, and received the reply, 'I have a little brother at home who is sick'. Mr. Repp then asked me to take him to the little girl's home, and saw to it that the sick brother also received something to eat."

One of the most interesting men whom Repp met during his stay in Russia was Philip Knies, the former schoolteacher in Schilling. Mr. Knies was then 79 years old, but in spite of his age, still had an unusually keen mind, and Mr. Repp always found it a great pleasure to carry on a conversation with the old gentleman. In a letter dated February twelve, he gave the following excellent summary of the background of the famine and the opening of the A. R. A. kitchens.

> "The causes of the present food shortage in the Volga valley are the bad harvests of the last two years and the devastating effects of the Civil War. As a result of these two factors the amount of grain and livestock in the villages began to decrease so rapidly that in the summer of 1921 a struggle for our very existence began. In order to secure sufficient food for our families, we began to sell our furniture, clothing, bedding, etc., to those people in the cities who still possesed more wealth than we. This money was then used to buy a few provisions in the markets. We also gathered various herbs in the forests and fields as well as potato plants and potato peelings. Skinny horses, which were too weak for field work, were killed and eaten. In the wake of the famine, epidemics also broke out and began to kill off children as well as adults. The village of Schilling which has only 3,000 inhabitan's, lost 300 people in 1921, and an additional 59 have died since New Year.

> "Thousands of our German people, who had relatives in the United States tried to **rescue** themselves by fleeing from Russia. They got rid of their few remaining possessions and set out hopefully for America. Their more sen-

sible neighbors warned them that this was impossible, but all such advice fell upon deaf ears. Some of them were gone only a short time when they got discouraged and returned to their former villages in a penniless condition. The largest number, however, continued on their way until they reached the Russian border. There some of them still sit, using up the last of their remaining money. Others have since died, leaving their children alone and unprotected.

"However, just when our distress had reached its greatest peak, and famine stared us all in the face, the A. R. A. appeared. The men in charge seemed like rescuing angels as they made preparations to open the first kitchen. At first only 250 children were fed, but this number was increased to 800 on December 14th, and we now hope to add an additional 150 next week. The village of Schilling would like to thank all of you for what you have done."

Rev. F. Wacker of Norka, who was always able to add interesting details of the relief work in his village, wrote a letter on December 19th in which he described some of the troubles of his committee:

"The most unpleasant thing about serving on the relief committee is that all of us are being criticized and gossiped about by some of the people of the village. If a committee member carries off a sack of empty cans in order to deliver them to the warehouse on the following day, somebody is certain to whisper, 'He's dragging half a sack of white bread home to his family'! The people who spread such tales the most energetically are naturally the ones whose own children were not chosen for the kitchen, and who are now poisoned by jealousy and anger.

"This has also been a period of trial for our cooks. They found it very difficult to prepare such large quantities of food, and sometimes the porridge was too thick and the next time too thin. A particularly severe headache was caused by the rice soup with butter dumplings. This soup tasted unusually good, but the dumplings swam on top, so that the first children who were served, received three or four dumplings, but the last children got none. Such injustice caused so much dissatisfaction that the cooks decided to use the rice for porridge entirely.

"The last month has also been a period of probation for our children. They were told on the day the kitchens opened that their names would be dropped for any act of misconduct. Until now this threat has had to be enforced only once. It occurred when a boy helped his mother steal some food. We are hoping that this one case will serve as a sufficient example.

"Finally the past month has been a period of trial for the whole village. At first only 500 children out of more than 2000 were fed. This caused a great deal of dissatisfaction, but the number has now been increased to 1000; so that practically every family is being helped. Some skeptics at first claimed that one meal a day couldn't make much difference anyway. But it is already possible to see the results of this meal. The children are beginning to get round checks again and a healthy facial color. Even their eyes and expressions have completely changed. And best of all, we have the irrefutable fact: 'Not a single child being fed in kitchens has died since the day they were opened, whereas, formerly the death rate among them was exceedingly high.' If you could have seen the miserable faces of the youngsters on November 14th, when they came for the first time, you would have realized clearly that they would all have died without the help of you people in America."

On March 13, 1922, John Gregg, one of the A. R. A. men from Moscow, came to Portland and addressed a meeting of the Volga Relief Society. In describing what the children were being fed, and why these particular foods were chosen, he stated:

"We fed cocoa and milk two days a week, and another two days we fed rice pudding, and on one day we served beans. A chunk of bread was given to the children with every meal. The other two days we generally fed corn grits, because it has a lot of fat in it and the children like it. So that was our menu. It seems when you speak of cocoa and white bread that they are quite a luxury, but such food is nutritous and it does not take up much room and is easy to ship. We use foods that have a lot of nourishment in them and will make a dish that anybody can eat. We feed about 218 grams which is really about all an adult can eat once a day; it is a big bowl of good food with a large piece of bread. We only feed once a day because it takes about five hours or sometimes six hours to get all the children through and to cook the meal and to clean up afterwards."

All of the letters that have been quoted so far were sent from the Bergseite, but before long messages began to arrive from the Wiesenseite as well. One of these came from Wiesenmüller and gave a summary of what had happened in the village since the beginning of the famine. The writer, Mr. Alexander Doell, tells us:

"Our crop in 1921 was a total failure, and as a result, flour was the first food product to disappear. The people then began to kill off their livestock, and when this failed, they had to subsist on beets, pumpkins, etc. Many of them crossed the river to the Bergseite hoping to find help there, but conditions on that side were equally bad. In their frantic fear they then sold their homes and possessions for practically nothing, or else drove off with wagon loads of furniture and farm implements which they later exchanged for a few pounds of fruit. In such cases some fled eastward and others westward, wherever a rumor told them that food was still on hand.

"At this time the government gave us a little help, but it made scarcely an impression on our great need; and we would have surely starved if America had not answered our cry of despair. We are told that the governor of Indiana gave the recommendation that this country come to our aid. May God reward him as well as all other Americans who took pity on our suffering.

"Just as 429 years ago the sailors with Christopher Columbus shouted, 'Land, Land!' as they approached the shores of the new world, so we joyfully cried, 'Bread, Bread'!, when the news came that a kitchen would be opened for the children. It is impossible to describe the happiness that shone in the faces of the youngsters as they sat down on November 27th for their first meal. They could scarcely believe that they were actually seeing the snow-white bread and the good rice porridge. Many of their parents who stood watching the scene had tears in their eyes as they silently prayed, 'May God be thanked for His great mercy'." (4).

Another letter written by Heinrich H. Weigand tells a similiar story for his village of Kukkus:

"The Volga valley has never seen such distress as existed after the crop failure of 1921. Before long our people began to swell with starvation. The death rate steadily increased and most of us had alreay given up all hope for the future. Finally we heard the story that America was coming to our help. Many people shook their heads unbelievingly that assistance could come from such a distant place. Finally on November 15 an American gentleman named Mr. Clapp arrived in our village and gave us the joyful news that half of our children in Kukkus between the ages of 0 and fifteen could eat in an A. R. A. kitchen once a day.

"Letters also began to arrive from friends and relatives that strengthened us in our will to live, because the messages always read, 'Don't despair. We're coming to your aid. Mass meetings are being held. Money is being collected. Rest assured: help is on the way'." (5).

In spite of the encouragement that the Volga Germans received by the opening of the first kitchens, their last food reserves gradually disappeared, and as the winter wore on, the number of people needing help became greater and greater. This condition was particularly bad after the first of February, and as a result, Mr. Jacob Suppes, the Soviet Commissar in Belzer, sent a written appeal to Mr. Repp for aid. His letter, which was dated February 14, pointed out the necessity of increasing the number of children being fed in the A.R.A. kitchens. He had previously believed that the statistics listing the percentage of starving children had been greatly exaggerated, but a more thorough investigation of conditions had convinced him of his error. He was now positive that the situation was far more terrible than he had ever imagined, and that in all villages there were daily deaths from starvation. His appeal ended with the words, "Therefore, I beg you once more, George, to do whatever lies in your power that the rations for children and for sick adults be increasd. It would also be wise if you tried to get the supplies for the next six weeks loaded immediately, because you know how slowly everything moves."

Mrs. George Repp was also the recipient of a very touching letter written by Rev. Edward Eichhorn of Alt-Messer, who made the following plea for the children of the German villages:

> "If you could see our suffering and our misery, dear Mrs. Repp, you would surely break into tears. Our whole world has become a great valley of unhappiness; and your husband is our only source of strength. For that reason do not ask him to return to America. Let him remain with us for still a little while, because he has become our father and we are all his children. He has adopted an innumerable throng of children, and you, as his wife, have become the mother of these hungry children. We are all praying that you, as our mother, will open up your heart to us, and call upon your countrymen to help in our distress. May our God, who is also the God of America, strengthen you in your work so that you will not become weary in carrying out the great task that lies in your hands."

We may rest assured that Mr. Repp was just as anxious as Jacob Suppes and Rev. Eichhorn to put more of his "adopted children" into the kitchens. The proof for this lies in the fact that on February 24th an additional 10,000 children were able to enter the Bergseite kitchens, so that the number of boys and girls receiving a daily meal was now 40,000 instead of the former 30,000 of January 1st.

However, in spite of this constant increase in child-feeding, there were several periods when it became necessary for some of the kitchens to close their doors for a short time. At least three different factors were responsible for this situation. The first was that the Baltic Sea and the Kiel Canal froze so hard in February and March that no ships could get through to bring the necessary supplies for the thousands of kitchens that were operating in Russia. It was said at the time that the Baltic had not frozen so badly in twenty-five years and the Kiel Canal was never known to have frozen before.

Then after the spring thaws came, the roads became such miry passages that in many parts of Russia it was impossible for wagons to reach the warehouses in which the food was stored. As Fisher expressed it, "The whole country became a sea of black tenacious mud, which for a period of two weeks or a month held up communication as effectively as an inundation." (6)

The third problem, which was a constant source of worry to the A. R. A. men, was the transportation system in Russia. Ever since the beginning of the World War the railroads had been allowed to deteriorate to such an extent that by 1921 they were in a deplorable condition. Even when food did arrive in the Baltic and Black Sea ports, it often had to lie in these towns for weeks at a time, until enough freight cars could be sent to carry it away. The Soviet government had promised the A. R. A. when it entered Russia that from 400-500 cars would be supplied daily at the ports of entry. This number was later reduced to 250, but even that was more than the railroads could deliver, and while telegrams poured in from the feeding districts asking for more and more food, Soviet officials came with the discouraging news that only 160 cars could be spared. This situation was especially bad by the end of March, when nearly 60,000 tons of American relief supplies were in storage at the various ports.

After the food trains left the coast, they crawled with "maddening deliberation" towards the hungry people of the famine areas. The first train carrying supplies from the Black Sea to Ufa arrived after many

— 70 —

weeks of wandering which took it over most of European Russia. After hearing the story of its travels, the district supervisor of that city wired the Port Representative that it might be wise to equip future trains with a sextant, a compass, and a map of the world! Additional difficulties were caused by the condition of the engines. Patched and battered wrecks were dragged from repair shops and were turned over to an underfed train crew whose lack of interest in their work helped to cause the disappearance of one-third of the A. R. A. trains by the end of January. It was finally necessary for the Americans to set up their own checking system which eventually reduced the number of "missing" trains to one-eighth of one per cent. (7).

Then when the A. R. A. food reached such distribution centers as Samara, Saratov, Simbirsk, etc., there still remained the task of forwarding it to the rural areas where the kitchens were located. The Soviet government soon realized that this second problem was causing even more difficulty than the first, and in an attempt to remedy the situation, sent transportation officials to all the areas in which the A. R. A. was located. In Saratov a man by the name of Alexander Beerman was given complete jurisdiction over rail and water transportation, repairs, gasoline, labor, fuel, etc. At first it was thought that these measures would bring a little order out of the general chaos, but according to Mr. Fisher in his book "The Famine in Soviet Russia", all such hopes were quickly disillusioned. We are told that Mr. Beerman was far more interested in espionage and in getting his own men appointed on the various committees connected with the relief work, than in actually being helpful to the Americans located in Saratov. As a result, Mr. Repp, as well as all the other men had to constantly contend with the inefficiency and delay of both Comrade Beerman and the satellites in his office. (8).

When one considers all of these circumstances, it is not surprising to read in a letter, written on March 22nd by Philip Knies that a message had just been received in Schilling ordering the Food Committee to reduce the children's portions to one-half the usual

amount. Mr. Knies laments that although the youngsters had been able to get along on this one meal a
day, he doubts if a half portion would be sufficient to
keep them alive, since many of them got absolutely
nothing to eat at home.

In spite of these emergency measures, all of the
food in the Schilling warehouse was eventually used,
and by the middle of April the kitchen had to close
down entirely. It is easy to imagine the despair that
was felt by both the children and their parents when
the last meal was served and how anxiously they stood
on the bluff overlooking the river as they waited hope-
fully for Mr. Repp and his barge from Saratov.

The sight which greeted the Americans when they
finally did arrive reminded Mr. Repp of the day in November when he came down the Volga bringing his
first shipment of food. Mr. Knies describes the scene
in the following picturesque fashion:

> "April 29th will always be remembered in Schilling as
> a time of great thanksgiving because finally after a per-
> iod of long waiting and almost hopeless despair, a bright
> day finally dawned for the starving people of our village.
> At ten o'clock this morning a steamer, accompanied by a
> barge, entered our harbor bringing 40,000 poods of differ-
> ent American products for the children's kitchens. The
> news soon spread from house to house, and the entire
> population of the town—men, women and children, rushed
> to the wharf. As soon as they saw the boat, they all knelt
> down, and as tears of joy streamed down their faces, they
> sang one song after another expressing their happiness
> and gratitude.
>
> "Then the task of unloading began, and everyone — men
> and women as well as the old people, insisted upon helping.
> Many of them were in a weakened and half-starved condi-
> tion, but they all did their share in carrying the boxes of
> food to the shore.
>
> "Mr. Repp and Rev. Wagner, who had come with the
> ship, directed the unloading and also assisted in the actual
> work. In the evening Mr. Repp announced that everyone
> who had helped was to receive a meal consisting of some
> soup and rice porridge."

The letter goes on to tell that there were approximately 58,000 children between the ages of 0 to fifteen
living on the Bergseite at this time, and that from now
on 54.040 children were to receive a daily meal in the

A. R. A. kitchens. The food itself was to be distributed from three Volga warehouses in the following way:

Schilling warehouses for Balzer Rayon	21,350
Schilling warehouse for Franker Rayon	12,550
Nischnaja Bannowka warehouse for Kamenwa Rayon	8,700
Nischnaja Dobrinka warehouse for Dobrinka Rayon	11,440
Total children	54,040

These statistics prove that after the first of May, the famine was completely broken—as far as the children were concerned—since practically all of them were now being fed by the A. R. A., and the few who were not included could be taken care of by their parents. A similar report was made at this time by the Americans on the Wiesenseite of the river who were also able to provide for all the children who needed assistance. However, there still remained the problem of the adult population, which will be discussed in the following chapters.

FOOTNOTES

1. H. H. Fisher, **op. cit.**, 557.
2. This report was sent to Mr. Miller by the A. R. A. office on Jan- 24, 1922.
3. **Volga Relief Society Bulletin**, January 27, 1922.
4. From a letter written on February 27, 1922.
5. From a letter written on May 18, 1922.
6. H. H. Fisher, **op. cit.**, 219.
7. **Ibid**, 183-188.
8. **Ibid**, 117-130.

Chapter Five.

RAISING MONEY IN THE UNITED STATES.

The fact has already been mentioned that as early as September 2, 1921, the Volga Relief Society had received $40,433.24 from the following states:

Oregon	$16,736.88
California	16,692.34
Washington	4,792.31
Nebraska	1,190.77
Oklahoman	279.00
South Dakota	30.00
Colorado	22.00
	$40,433.24

In addition, enough subscriptions had been raised so that the society was assured of receiving at least $73,552.68 during the coming months. In some cases the Volga Germans had a little difficulty in immediately forwarding their money to Portland. This was particularly true in Colorado where the people are engaged in the sugar beet industry and receive their checks from the factories after the delivery of their crops. However, as soon as the money was on hand, the amounts which they had pledged were sent to Portland, and eventually $17,829.50 was received from this state alone.

Throughout the winter of 1921-1922 Mr. Miller continued the practice of writing circular letters in which he sent up-to-date reports on the progress of the work both in the United States and in Russia. For example, many of the previously quoted letters telling of the opening of the kitchens were first published in these weekly circulars. Thus the American people were kept in constant touch with the relief operations in Russia. Ordinarily over one hundred letters were sent to interested communities in twenty different states of the union.

At first these circulars were written in the English

language, but so many requests for German letters began to arrive that after September 27th they were sent out in both languages. Two of the questions that Mr. Miller was often asked were: (1) Are you positive that our money will reach the proper place, and (2) can we designate that a contribution is to go to a particular family? These questions were answered in the following manner:

"In becoming connected with the American Relief Administration we knew that there was not a more reliable source through which we could work. The United States government does its work through them, and if our government relies upon this organization, we know that we can, especially with a man like Herbert Hoover at the head of it.

"Before leaving New York, Mr. Repp advised us that the American Relief Administration already had great quantities of food in Russia, and, in fact, heading toward our colonies. They did not even wait for us to send the money with which to buy these supplies, and as soon as Mr. Repp arrives, he will have a large amount of food to distribute among our people.

"In answer to the second question, we are not accepting contributions to any one family, but a person may designate the colony to which his money should go. When our Mr. Repp gets into a colony he wants to feed the hungry regardless of who they are . . . If your families are not suffering and their neighbors are, it would not be right to turn food or money over to them and let the neighors starve." (1).

During this early period, while the plans of both the A. R. A. and the Volga Relief Society were still in a formative stage, two problems arose that required a little time and patience in solving. As soon as the German-Russian people in the United States realized how serious the famine was, they were very anxious to send boxes of clothing and food directly to their adult relatives. This seemed especially necessary after they heard that the A. R. A. would carry on child feeding only. Mr. Repp discussed both of these problems with the men in the New York office, and was informed that the A. R. A. could make no promises regarding the sending of used clothing, but that it was discussing the matter of adult feeding with the Soviet government, and hoped to introduce what it called the Food Draft System. This would mean that an American citizen could send ten dollars to New York, and the A. R. A. would deliver a package of food for that amount to any person who might be designated.

In a letter dated September 24, Mr. Miller informed his readers of the news that he had received. He said in part:

"From New York Mr. Repp advised us that as yet we cannot send clothing. Therefore, do not ship anything to us until you hear more definite news. However, get your things together and be ready to send them just as soon as we pass the word to you, as we do not want to lose any time when the doors are opened for clothing. In packing be careful of the moths. Either fumigate the clothes or use plenty of moth balls. More clothes were ruined by the moths than lost in transit when they were sent to other countries."

The solution of the clothing problem was finally suggested by Mr. Frank Page of the A. R. A. office when he telegraphed on October 26th:

"Regarding clothing do not believe it will be possible through ourselves or any other relief or religious organization to deliver specific packages to individuals in Russia. Lutherans and Quakers instituting clothing appeal for general clothing distribution in Russian district, but cannot guarantee that it will go into one district or to any individual. Recommend that your people support either of these organizations in their general clothing campaign, as need of old clothing very great. American Relief Administration clothing operations entirely confined to purchases of new clothing and its distribution among the needy."

As a result of this advice, Mr. Miller immediately got in touch with Dr. Lauritz Larsen of the National Lutheran Council, who assured him that clothing would be distributed among the Volga German people "to the best of their ability." This news was then included in the next circular letter sent to the branches, many of whom already had their boxes packed for shipment.

The people of Portland also got to work and during the next two months sent five tons of clothing to the New York office of the National Lutheran Council. The first shipment of twenty-two boxes included $1000.00 of new material which the local Ladies Aid had sewed into garments. The second shipment consisted of 6636 pounds contributed by the Volga Relief Societies of Fresno. California; Ritzville, Washington; and Endicott, Washington.

Numerous letters from the secretaries of many other branches began to arrive telling of boxes that were being sent directly to New York. It is impossible to mention all of these correspondents, but they included Rev. Richard Otto of Calgary, Alberta, Canada; Mr. George Fahrenbruch of Culbertson, Nebraska; and Rev. Anhorn of Billings, Montana. In addition there was Rev. F. Bremecke of Montrose, Colorado, whose little community sent 1,114 pounds of clothing and shoes; Rev. L. C. Boeker of Denver, who told that the Ladies Aid of his church included $400.00 of new clothing in their shipment; Rev. A. Grabener of Walla Walla, Washington, whose branch collected between 2000 and 3000 pounds of clothing and shoes; and Rev. J. G. Eckhardt of Odessa, whose outstanding organization alone shipped 10,481 pounds of clothing to the National Lutheran Council via Seattle.

The second problem regarding the sending of Food Drafts also took time in solving. For an entire month the A. R. A. carried on negotiations with the Soviet government, until finally on October 17 all arrangements were completed and the American people ' were informed that it would be possible for them to send a ten-dollar food package to a definite beneficiary. It was stated that the package would contain eight of the following commodities: flour, bacon, lard, vegetable oil, tea, canned milk, hominy, sugar, cocoa, rice and beans. All remittances were sent to the A. R. A. headquarters in Moscow from where they were forwarded to the American warehouse located in the recipient's neighborhood. The person to whom the draft had been sent was then notified to come to the warehouse and receive his supplies. (2).

It is easy to imagine the feeling of relief among the German-Russian people in the United States upon hearing that such an agreement had been made. At various times in the preceding weeks the A. R. A. had expressed a doubt that the Volga Relief Society's plan of designating part of their money for specific colonies would prove practical; but Mr. Miller wrote in a circular letter dated October 26th:

"This Food Draft System now removes every obstacle in the way of definitely getting every cent contributed for a certain colony spent in that colony, and also provides for help being sent direct to one's own family. All money contributed here in Portland and sent us by our branches will be handled exactly as requested. A blanket draft will be sent to each colony designated; and the General Fund, which is the largest of all, will be spent in those German colonies needing help the most."

As soon as the blanks for the Food Remittance System were received in Portland, Oregon, the Volga German people of that city were notified of their arrival. In order to facilitate the filling out of the drafts, Mrs. Repp announced that she would be glad to help with this task and also to forward the money to New York. Since the name and address of the recipient had to be written in both the English and the Russian language, a man by the name of George H. Mueller, who had been a former schoolteacher in Russia, would come to her home and perform the latter task. These drafts were to prove so popular that by December 5, 1922, $29,190 had been sent in this form by the Portland people alone.

The efficiency with which the Volga Relief Society had been organized and the fine leadership of its officers were acknowledged by Mr. Frank Page in a letter dated November 23, 1921, in which he said:

"We should like to congratulate you upon the fact that yours is the only organization to date that has gone to work and collected funds, sent them to Russia and is having food distributed without a delay of any kind. We appreciate the confidence you had in us in working first and finding out afterwards, and we feel certain that because of this your people in the Volga district have been more quickly served than people of any other group who may have relatives in the United States:

Another letter from Mr. Page which was received with justifiable pride in Portland, was dated December 9, and stated:

"Governor Goodrich returned last Saturday and I had a very pleasant and interesting talk with him. He told me that he had spent a week with Mr. Repp going through the German colonies and unquestionably the condition in these colonies was worse than any in Russia; that the German people were by far the most capable of all in that district and that it was very touching to see the gratitude that they felt toward the American people as a whole, but more particularly toward their kin in this country, who had thought of them in their distress. He said that Mr. Repp is one of the most welcome Americans in Russia because he brings tangible word from their families and people here. Sending him there has been a great asset and from every report we can get, he is the right man for the job."

These messages from the American Relief Administration were naturally read with great interest by the people most responsible for the success of the Volga Relief Society, and did much to compensate them for the many hours of tedious work that they had spent at their tasks. It is also fortunate that such moments of satisfaction did come to Mr. Miller and Mrs. Repp, because during the next months many vexatious incidents arose that caused them a certain amount of worry and annoyance. One of these was in connection with the news that Mr. Repp was to feed the children on the Bergseite only, whereas Mr. Paul Clapp had been given the Wiesenseite. A large number of the people living in Fresno came from the east side of the river, and upon hearing that Mr. Repp would not open kitchens in their villages, some of them began to fear that their relatives were being neglected by the Volga Relief Society.

As a result, it was necessary for Mr. Miller to reassure them constantly that feeding was progressing with the same amount of speed in both groups of colonies, and that there was no cause for alarm. In California it was pointed out, however, that during the early winter months practically all of the letters from Russia telling about the opening of the kitchens came from the Bergseite. This was unfortunately true, although there was a very simple explanation. Mr. Repp naturally sent frequent reports of his work to Portland, and also requested the pastors of the village that were in his district to write lengthy detailed accounts of what had occurred. Paul Clapp, on the other hand, was under no obligation to notify anyone except the Moscow office of his activities.

Eventually, of course, the California people heard from their relatives that they were being given the same amount of care that the colonies on the other side of the river were receiving; and even the greatest critics finally saw the wisdom in the A. R. A.'s using two men in the German villages rather than just one.

Another unfortunate incident arose in connection with the matter of adult feeding. It is probably true that even today many German-Russians in America fail to realize how much of the work carried on in the Volga colonies was paid for by the American Relief Administration and not by themselves. For example, when the first money from Portland was sent to New York, part of these funds were intended for child feeding in the German villages. But after the Food Drafts were introduced, the A. R. A. very generously agreed to bear the entire cost of this phase of their work, and even returned to the Volga Relief Society the money that had already been used. As a result, every cent of the contributions raised by the German-Russian people was put aside in a separate fund which was later distributed among all the inhabitants of the colonies designated by the donors. However, it took some time until sufficient food was on hand in Russia for this to be accomplished, and consequently, during the months of November and December child-feeding only was carried on.

In the meantime a great deal of disappointment and impatience was being expressed in the United States at the news that no adults were being assisted. A German newspaper entitled the "California Post", which represented a small minority opinion, even stated that "had the people of California known that only children would be fed, not one cent would have been sent to Portland from California." This comment evoked a sharp retort from Mr. Miller, "I wonder whom the "California Post" thinks these children belong to? Think of it, not one cent for our brothers' and sisters' children! They are evidently expected to starve." (3).

In addition, Volga Germans in America who had sent packages of food through such private concerns as A. Fink and Sons wrote to their relatives telling them of gifts that were on the way. Occasionally these people believed that the packages had been sent to the A. R. A., and the dissatisfied letters which they sent back to the United States, when the men at the warehouses were unable to help them, were often misinterpreted here.

There was also a brief period in which the Americans in Russia seemed to misunderstand just how the Volga Relief Society money was to be distributed, and their lack of information naturally added to the confusion. This situation finally caused Mr. Miller so much concern that on January 14 he wired the full details to Mr. Page and requested that the matter be clarified more definitely. Within a few hours the following reply was received in Portland:

"Have cabled your wire in full to Moscow and added following — 'Have cabled repeatedly and written that this Volga Relief money for bulk relief. Give us definite assurance that food against this money is going to adults as well as children in Volga colonies. Will follow this through until have definite assurance money is going as we have ordered and you desire. Feel certain that this has been straightened out over month ago in Russia."

Mr. Page was, of course, correct in his supposition, and eventually it became evident that a great many people had been unnecessarily alarmed over the situation. On January 28th their fears were definitely allayed when a cable arrived saying: "Repp wires from Saratov he is already feeding adults in Goloi Karamisch Uyesd and will expand adult feeding rapidly as possible."

It might be mentioned in passing that whenever a vexatious situation of this kind arose, it was handled by the men in the New York office with the utmost tact, patience, and diplomacy. Because of the very urgency of the relief work it was probably inevitable that moments of friction should arise among the thousands of German-Russians who were so keenly interested in what was being done. However, in going through the correspondence of the A. R. A., it is impossible to find a single letter which is lacking in sympathy and understanding. As Mr. Page himself once tolerantly stated, "It is over-enthusiasm and a lack of knowledge of the facts which quite often causes unfortunate situations to arise."

It should also be said that throughout its entire history the Volga Relief Society and the American Relief

Administration remained on the friendliest of terms, and that the officials of the two organizations constantly supported each other to the best of their ability.

Although temporary annoyances did arise, the work of the society continued to progress in an amazing fashion. It would be impossible to repeat all the details listed in the monthly financial reports that were sent out, but in summarized form we notice that the money sent to New York steadily rose in the following manner:

September 21	$ 40,433.24
October 31	66,297.83
December 1	86,094.84
January 1	88,682.92
March 10	98,920.93
May 13	100,448.00
December 8	110,848.28

Since the report on December 8, 1922 marked the end of the Volga Relief Society as a separate organization, the detailed statement issued on that date is included:

STATEMENT OF DECEMBER 8, 1922.

Oregon

Portland	$29,576.86
Salem	15.00
Ruckles	15.00

California

Fresno	24,242.33
Lodi	1,544.15
Burbank	100.00
Anaheim	5.00
Bischoff	5.00

Washington

Endicott	1,415.50
Walla Walla	2,456.95
Ritzville	2,384.00
Odessa	4,184.83
Dryden	1,203.51
Tacoma	597.50
Waterville	930.00
Quincy	418.60
Farmington	109.50
Sunnyside	20.00
Alkali Flats	315.00
Ralston	154.50
Seattle	120.55
Wapato	50.00

Warden	206.75
Snoqualamie	50.00
Wilkinson	12.50
Blaine	15.00

Canada

Calgary	692.84
Irvine	42.00
Hilda	431.65
Trochu	674.13
Duffield	85.50
Castor	156.00
Martins	124.91
Hanna	98.50
Stony Plain	261.00
Duchess	46.00
Rosemary	24.00
Leader	600.88
Hatton	64.00
Estuary	2.40
Winnipeg	762.04

Oklahoma

Manitou	279.00
Weatherford	1,298.75
O'Keene	10.00
Fargo	25.00

Nebraska		**New Ulm**	12.60
Lincoln	190.77	Northfield	20.00
Alliance	20.00	**South Dakota**	
Culbertson	2,521.30	Redfield	38.10
McCook	3,062.80	Greenway	30.00
Sutton	214.84	Alpena	76.00
Colorado		Tripp	10.00
Ft. Collins	2,325.31	**North Dakota**	
Brush	2,621.20	Elliott	58.00
Ft. Morgan	2,928.50	Willa	10.00
Sterling	3,833.25	Kermit	4.60
Denver	4,485.00	Elgin	10.00
Montrose	1,491.24	Heil	35.00
Windsor	25.00	**New York**	
Grover	50.00	Pine Island	1,081.00
Kendrick	5.00	**Idaho**	
Julesburg	65.00	American Falls	144.65
Montana		Parker	126.13
Billings	3,540.35	Paul	10.40
Laurel	425.00	**Kansas**	
Plevna	141.00	Herrington	112.00
Forsyth	50.00	Ramona	1,370.00
Sidney	84.75	LaCrosse	20.00
Hardin	136.75	Learned	40.50
Chinook	20.00	**Wyoming**	
Watkins	27.65	Worland	151.00
Wisconsin		Ucross	25.00
Fond du lac	806.00	**Iowa**	
Oshkosh	618.50	Mason City	100.90
Illinois		Council Bluffs	2.00
Naperville	5.00	**Massachusetts**	
Chicago	10.00	Boston	5.00
Michigan		**South America**	
Flint	1,186.00	Argentina	243.76
Saginaw	602.50		
Minnesota		Total	$110,848.28
St. Paul	165.00		
St. Peters	15.30		

In addition to the $110,000.00 actually handled by the men in Portland, a further sum of $21,500.00 should be credited to their organization. This is to be explained by the fact that in order to save time, several of the Volga Relief Society branches sent either all or part of their money directly to New York. The people of Fresno, for example, forwarded $15,760.00 to the A. R. A. for the outright purchase of food, which was divided equally among all the people of thirteen colonies on the

Wiesenseite. Consequently, Fresno's total contribution consisted of $37,482.33, which reflects both the great generosity of its people, and the outstanding ability of such hard-working leaders as Andrew Wolf, William Kerner, Conrad Klein, John Lung, H. P. Steitz, etc. (4).

Two other communities that wished to save time by mailing their checks immediately to the A. R. A. were N. Milwaukee, Wis., and Chicago, Illinois. The branch society in the former city chose Rev. Günther as its president, and under his leadership raised $781.00. This information was at once forwarded to Mr. Miller and was included in the reports of the branches.

The organization of the Volga Germans in Chicago took place on September 7, 1921. At that meeting Rev. Adolf Niedergesäss was chosen president, and Rev. F. G. Mertins, secretary. On the following day they informed Mr. Miller:

"Last evening we organized in Jefferson Park an 'Unter-stützungs-Verein für die Wiesenseite' since all of our people came from that part of Russia. We intend to be a branch of your society and to work through your representative, Mr. Repp. As we have about 1000 German-Russian families living in and about Chicago, we hope that our organization will prove a success."

The zeal shown by both the officers and the various committees chosen to solicit funds in the German churches, resulted in the raising of $7,500.00 for the famine-sufferers of the Volga valley.

Two other organizations worked entirely independent of Portland. They were the so-called Rocky Mountain Society and the Central States Volga Relief Society. The first group consisted primarily of four Colorado towns: Greeley, Windsor, Loveland, and Berthoud. These communities chose Rev. J. H. Ament of Greeley as their president and during the following months sent $6,609.13 to the American Relief Administration. In later years, after a union of all the societies took place, two Greeley members, Mr. Fred Brug and Mr. Conrad Koehler were to be of great assistance as national officers. (5).

Although this book is intended to tell primarily the story of the Portland Volga Relief Society, it is impossible to omit mentioning again the outstanding work of the independent Lincoln organization. Reference has already been made to the fact that the Central State's contribution of $70,100.00 was an important part of the $220,000.00 which was distributed in Russia. (6) In addition to this sum, the Lincoln people also gave $9,696.00 to the American Volga Relief Society that was organized in November, 1922. (7). Thus we see that approximately $80,000.00 was raised between September 11, 1921, when the society was organized, and November 4, 1922, when the national union took place.

Of this total sum $26,500.00 was contributed by the Volga Germans of Lincoln, and $12,000.00 by Americans who responded to a "Drive" that was held in the city in February. (8). Thirty thousand dollars came from other Nebraska towns such as Hastings, Harvard, Grand Island, Scottsbluff, and Sutton, which were branches of the society. (The files of the society reveal that part of this amount was sent to Lincoln in response to a "State Drive" that took place in April.) An additional $12,000.00 came from five other states, the most important of which was Kansas. (9).

In order to raise this sum of money, a great deal of work had to be done by both the officers of the Central States Society, as well as by the members of the Board of Directors and by the leaders of the various branches affiliated with the Lincoln group. A few of the men who were especially active in this connection were Rev. J. Rothenberger of Scottsbluff, Mr. Henry Hein of Hastings, Mr. Henry Stroh of Grand Island, and Mr. John Jeckel of Newark, New Jersey. The people of Hastings probably contributed more money than any other Nebraska community outside of Lincoln. As early as September 23, 1921, Mr. Hein was able to report that the Volga Germans of his city had subscribed $3000.00 for the Relief Fund, and in March, 1922, an additional $2,562.16 was raised in a house-to-house canvas of the entire city. (10).

However, it must not be assumed that the figures quoted above represent the total amount of money contributed by the various Volga Relief Societies. We have heard that in Portland alone $29,190.00 was sent to Russia in the form of Food Drafts, and from all indications the response in other cities was similarly generous. But because of the fact that this money was forwarded directly to New York, it is impossible to give accurate statistics on the amount of money sent by the various Volga German communities. In a letter written on March 8, 1922, William Kerner, the secretary of the Fresno society, informed Mr. Miller that he knew personally of $14,430.00 that had been forwarded from his city. However, this was only four months after the introduction of the Remittance System, and it was to continue in operation for another year. Furthermore, many Fresno people sent their money from banks or were assisted by other members and officers of the society, such as Mr. H. P. Steitz.

In going through Mr. Miller's correspondence, it is possible to find a few additional comments on this subject. Mr. George Fahrenbruch of Culbertson, Nebraska, who was one of the most methodical of all the branch secretaries, sent detailed monthly statements to Portland, and thus we learn that between December, 1921, and July, 1922, he was asked to forward $1495.00 in Food Drafts. Conrad Scheideman, the capable secretary in McCook, Nebraska, told that by April 24, 1922, the members of his organization had given $1440.00 for the same purpose. And on April 24, 1922, Rev. J. G. Eckhardt reported that he personally had written $1110.00 worth of Food Drafts for the people of Odessa, Washington, but that an additional $300.00 or $400.00 had been sent to New York without his assistance.

However, at the present time the only complete statistics are those which Mrs. George Repp has kept for the people of Portland, Oregon. In her city the amount of money given to both General Feeding and to Food Drafts was practical equal. In each case it consisted of $29,000.00. If these figures can be taken as a criteria for the other communities connected with the Volga Relief Societies, it would be reasonable to suppose that an additional $220,000.00 was raised in this manner. The American Relief Administration evidently shares this opinion, because in Rev. G. J. Schmidt's interesting pamphlet entitled "Bericht der American Volga Relief

Society" we read that Mr. Page credited the various organizations with having contributed approximately $200,000.00 in this form. (11).

But the entire story is still not given unless one mentions many boxes of new and used clothing which were sent to Russia. We have already heard that during the winter of 1921-1922 much of this was sent through the auspices of the National Lutheran Council, but a more satisfactory way, which was carried out by the Central States Volga Relief Society, will be discussed in another chapter. It is naturally very difficult to make an estimate of the financial value of used clothing, but it would be reasonable to suppose that at the very least, these various shipments amounted to another $100,000.00.

Additional sums of money were spent in sending private packages of food and clothing to the people of Russia by means of the postal service. A very large percentage of these packages either failed to arrive or came with many of the contents stolen, but they all represented a financial sacrifice on the part of the donor. Then too, many of the branches connected with the Volga Relief Societies sent money for Volga refugees to the German Red Cross, or contributed to the funds raised by Rev. John Schleuning and other lecturers who visited their communities. In a letter published in the "Welt Post" on January 25, 1923, Rev. Schleuning mentions $10,000.00 which he alone had collected. Rev. G. F. Schmidt also tells us that between 1922 and 1924 the American Volga Relief Society sent $28,146.05 to Russia for various charitable activities. (12). When one considers all of these factors, it is easy to see that a minimum sum of $550,000.00 can be credited to the people of the Volga Relief Societies.

However, in order to get a complete picture of all the relief work carried on by the 120,000 Volga Germans living in the United States, the reader should be reminded that a great deal of additional money was raised by charitable societies which appealed to definite religious groups. Many German-Russians are Mennonites, Catholics, Baptists, etc., and in all of these churches money was raised and distributed by the various denominations concerned. Another very important organization was the National Lutheran Council, whose outstanding work in Russia has already been mentioned. The people who affiliated with these religious organizations also packed boxes of clothing and sent large sums of money to their relatives in the form of Food Drafts. Consequently, it is not difficult to believe that between the years 1921-1923 the Volga Germans of the United States raised more than one million dollars for their kinsmen in Russia. This phenomenal figure shows not only the great generosity and sympathy of these people, but also the unusual thrift and industry which they had shown in the new world. If this had not been the case, such an enormous contribution would have been impossible. (13).

FOOTNOTES

1. **Volga Relief Society Circular,** Sept. 27, 1921.
2. H. H. Fisher, **op. cit.,** 514-522.
3. **Volga Relief Society Circular,** March 10, 1922.
4. The money sent to New York is mentioned by William Kerner in a letter dated March 8, 1922.
5. The funds from No. Milwaukee, Chicago, Colorado and the $904.00 mentioned in footnote 6 are given in the **Volga Relief Society Bulletin** of May 13, 1922. Additional sums may have been sent later.
6. The sum of $70,100 is given by G. J. Schmidt, **op. cit.,** 8. The $220,000.00 that the A. R. A. mentions in its book came from the following sources, as far as the author has been able to determine:

    Volga Relief Society with all its branches............$131,500.00
    Central States Volga Relief Society 70,100.00
    Rocky Mountain States Volga Relief Society...... 6,609.13
    Miscellaneous sources—sent to New York 904.00
    American Volga Relief Society (approximately) 10,000.00

    $219,113.13

    The remainder of the money spent by the American Volga Relief Society was given to the colonies after the A. R. A. left Russia.
7. **Minute Book of the American Volga Relief Society,** 23.
8. Letter written by Dr. H. P. Wekesser to Mr. Frank Page on February 16, 1922.
9. These figures were given by Mr. John Lebsock, the treasurer of the Central States Volga Relief Society, in November, 1922.
10. Mentioned in a letter to Dr. H. P. Wekesser on March 8, 1922.
11. G. J. Schmidt, **op. cit.,** 8
12. Ibid.
13. Richard Sallet, **op. cit.,** 101, estimates that more than two million dollars was sent to Russia during these years by the German people coming from all sections of the country. This would include the "Odessa", the Wolhynien, and other groups, all of whom sent aid to their friends and relatives.

Chapter Six.

THE CARE OF THE ADULTS — FOOD DRAFTS AND THE VOLGA RELIEF SOCIETY FUNDS.

The statement has already been made that during the early winter months many Volga Germans in the United States had difficulty in understanding why their parents and older relatives were not being fed. Mr. Repp tried to explain in all of his letters that there simply was not enough food to take care of both the children and the adults, but many Americans, in their failure to understand the many difficulties facing the A. R. A., felt that a miracle should be performed, and everyone taken care of immediately.

These people were later told that if Mr. Hoover's organization had not been conducting feeding operations in Europe during the post-war years, even the children could not have been fed as quickly as they were. What actually happened was that large supplies of food which were already in Europe were immediately transferred to Russia, so that on September 7, less than three weeks after the A. R. A. agreement with Litvinov was signed, kitchens had been established in Petrograd.

When Mr. Repp began his work in November, it might have been possible for him to divide the limited food at his disposal equally between all the inhabitants of his district, but that would have meant giving each person a few grams of rice or bread, and would have really benefited neither the children nor the parents. Consequently, it was decided to adopt the plan which was then put into operation; to pick out the very poorest children of the villages and feed them first. Then as more food came in, the number of youngsters receiving a daily meal could be gradually increased.

Although many German-Russians in America failed to realize it, this scheme actually aided the adults as well as the children. If a father and mother with four children had a small reserve of flour and potatoes left, and the children were fed in the A. R. A. kitchens, the parents, naturally, could keep all of their own food for themselves.

Another important factor was that the A. R. A. was paying for the supplies used in the childrens kitchens; so that if Mr. Repp had taken the Volga Relief Society funds and purchased the few products that were on hand, there would have been no free food left for the children. As it was, the society's money remained intact until the spring of the year when there were sufficient supplies to make an individual allocation to every man, woman, and child, in addition to what was being consumed in the kitchens.

Until the end of January there was only one way for the adult population to be taken care of immediately and that was through the Food Drafts. We have already heard that the Russian agreement which introduced this system was signed in October, but it took some time for the necessary details to be perfected. Consequently, the first Portland Food Draft was not written until November 10th. From the very start this scheme proved so popular that it became quite a problem to get all the orders immediately filled in Russia. and often more than six or eight weeks elapsed until the people along the Volga actually received the food.

The A. R. A. finally became so discouraged because of the difficulties that it was having with the Russian transportation system, that it decided to drop the entire project and return the money for undelivered packages to the original donor. A statement to that effect was prepared for release to the press on March 9, 1922. However, a more encouraging cable from Moscow arrived that very day, and it was decided to continue the work. (1). Later in the year when the Baltic was again open to transportation, the orders could be filled as soon as they came in. and Mr. Repp reported that as many as one thousand were given out each day in his area alone.

All drafts for the Volga Communes were forwarded to Saratov, where the clerks in the A. R. A. office would notify the recipient that the food was at his disposal. Since the smaller warehouses along the Volga were needed for the children's food, it was necessary for the people on both the Bergseite and Wiesenseite to come directly to Saratov. Long queues would form in front of the A. R. A. building set aside for this purpose, and as the people passed through the various departments, they were given a variety of different products. A ten-dollar draft enabled an individual to receive:

    49 pounds flour.
    25 pounds rice
    10 pounds lard or 9 pounds bacon.
    10 pounds sugar
    20 cans milk. (2).

Each recipient had to bring with him the A. R. A. notification card and also written proof that he was the person for whom the draft was intended. Relatives in America knew that in all the Volga villages many people bore the same last name, and often well-known nicknames would be added, in order that the right person would surely be reached. The phrase "Garte Krieger", for instance, identified one particular Krieger family whose home was surrounded by a beautiful orchard.

After the people received their supplies, they would usually return to their villages in large parties in order to protect each other on the homeward way. Food was very precious at this time, and there was always danger of a possible attack from bandits along the lonelier stretches of the road. None of the German-Russians had any guns with which they could defend themselves, and in spite of all precautions, frequent robberies and even an occasional murder occurred. An example of this kind took place when two young men from Norka were killed in a forest called "Kosakenwald", while bringing a sleigh of supplies to their village. (3).

In going through the letters sent from Russia to the Volga Relief Society, we find the first mention of Food Drafts in a message of gratitude from six inhabitants of Norka, who wrote on January 22nd:

"Although conditions in Norka get worse every day, we were greatly encouraged last Thursday when ten sleighs of provisions were brought to our village. Each of us received nine poods from our relatives in America. Many families who were on the verge of despair, have now been given new hope of being able to survive until the next harvest. We wish to thank everyone who helped in sending this food to us, and pray that God's richest blessings will reward them for what they have done."

On the same day Mr. Repp also reported:

"The personal Food Drafts are arriving in large numbers and are being filled as quickly as supplies come from Moscow. Transportation is in a terrible condition and is a constant source of worry. We are continually making plans which we are unable to carry out because of inadequate facilities."

Three weeks later Mr. Repp mentioned that a large number of drafts had arrived from the states of Oregon, Colorado, Nebraska, and California, and that he hoped transportation would soon be in better shape.

The most complete description of the happiness of the people in these food packages comes again from Rev. Wacker, who wrote the following letter dated March 15:

"Many people in America have been sending Food Drafts to their friends in Russia, but unfortunately our transportation system creates an unavoidable delay in the filling of these orders. Whenever a letter arrives telling of the purchase of one of these drafts, there usually follows a period of several weeks or even a month until the happy day when a 'Powestka' announces that the food is on hand. The fortunate possessors of these notices drive to Saratov to receive their packages. Then as the father returns contentedly with the precious food, everyone at home waits with burning impatience for his arrival.

"Finally the gate leading into the courtyard opens, and the whole household — old and young hurry out to welcome him. The packages are carried inside, and the joyful task of opening them begins. Each article seems more wonderful than the one before. In many cases the family had nothing at home except wheat husks, and now they see the most beautiful white flour. Formerly they were eating dried watermelon rinds and now they can make delicious rice porridge. You can imagine how welcome the lard and milk also is.

"On the same evening the samovar is brought out, and the first real pot of tea is made. It is impossible to mention all the substitutes that have been used in the past; apple and cherry leaves, roasted watermelon peelings and even carrot tops — anything that would discolor the water a little. And now the family drinks its first cup of delicious tea and can even add a teaspoon of sugar.

"A stranger would have to suffer the years of privation that lie behind us in order to understand our joy over the contents of these packages. For that reason I should like to call to all you: if you possibly can, send more Food Drafts to your friends. The happiness that is created by such a gift is simply indescribable. The drafts also constitute the only feasible way of helping your friends. A gift of ten dollars cash buys less than half of what we receive from the A. R. A. And if packages of food are sent directly from America, they usually disappear along the way. Even if they do arrive, the boxes have been opened and the contents stolen. Therefore, the only certain way of sending help is through the A. R. A. The transportation system is, of course, in a terrible condition. Many people receive letters from their friends that drafts are coming, but while they slowly starve, the food fails to arrive. And still I say again, 'Send money for your relatives and friends only in Food Drafts'."

The response to letters such as these was so great that eventually more than $700,000.00 in Food Drafts were distributed from the Saratov warehouse. (4). About sixty per cent of the people taken care of in this area were Russian, and the remaining forty per cent German. (5) but in Mr. Repp's opinion more than half of the Food Drafts were received by the German villages.

However, in the period between January 1 and March 9, when the railroad congestion was partially relieved, a steady stream of letters arrived in Portland with appeals for increased help. On New Year's day of 1922 Rev. Edward Eichhorn of Alt-Messer wrote:

"The 1200 children who are now being fed in the American kitchens send their utmost sincere thanks for the food which they receive. Their parents, however, look into the year 1922 with fearful hearts, and can only pray that their lives will be spared. In the past year 800 people in Messer died of starvation and an additional 400 left for other sections where they hoped to find bread. Alt-Messer now contains 3600 inhabitants as compared with its former population of 5000. Our people live on mere scraps of food; their clothing has been sold, and they lift their arms in despair to an unmerciful heaven.

"Prices are exorbitantly high; one pound of black bread costs 14,000 rubles; one pound of meat, 13,000 rubles; one pound of fresh butter 50,000 rubles; one cow, 3,000,000 rubles; one pair of oxen, 28,000,000 rubles, etc. These figures may give you some idea of our present struggles for existence."

At the same time Jacob Eichhorn, the schoolteacher in Bauer, was writing:

"Our poverty is unbelievably great. For months there has been no flour with which to make bread. The scraps that were formerly given to the pigs are now being eaten by human beings. If additional help does not come soon, large numbers of people will die of hunger. We often see beggars who wander from village to village with swollen faces and feet. Some of them are nothing but living skeletons. A famine as terrible as this has never been experienced before by the Volga Germans."

The village of Moor which has already been mentioned as one of the poorest in the entire German-Russian area was also in need of additional help. The condition of the people was especially bad in February when Albert Klein, the schoolteacher, sent the following appeal in the name of the entire village:

"The relief work which is being done in Moor is far from sufficient. Everything that we possess has already been eaten and universal starvation faces us all. It is impossible to describe our suffering and despair, except to say that we all join in the cry, 'Send us help! In God's name send us help!"

Appeals such as these also arrived daily in Mr. Repp's Balzer office, and it is easy to imagine his feeling of helplessness in being unable to immediately fulfull such requests. In spite of his impatience to begin distributing Volga Relief Society funds, it was necessary to wait until January 22 before sufficient food was on hand for such a purpose.

At that time he was able to obtain from ten to fifteen small freight cars of food, and with these, the first individual allotments consisting of lard, flour, and grits, were given to every man, woman and child in thirty-three German colonies. The plans for the distribution of this food had been made far in advance, so that no time was wasted after the supplies were on hand. We have already heard that a large part of the Volga Relief Society funds had been designated for invidual colonies. In such cases it was very simple to fulfill the wishes of the donors, but a much greater problem was caused by the distribution of $88,000.00 which had been placed in a general fund.

In order to be positive that the money would be sent where it was most needed, Mr. Repp sent a lengthy questionnaire to every village on both sides of the river.

CHILD FEEDING STATION IN MOOR.

In this document he asked for the population statistics for the three previous years, as well as the harvest yield, and the number of horses, sheep, cattle, etc. that the village possessed during the same period. The percentage of deaths from starvation, based upon the total population of the colony, was then carefully computed, and thus conclusions could be reached regarding the relative poverty of the different villages. If for any reason the figures seemed exaggerated, some of the A. R. A. assistants were sent to make a personal investigation. Mr. Repp also compared his information with that of the Soviet government, and discussed the allocation of food with Mr. John Ellingston in the A. R. A. Saratov office.

Since the information on conditions came from so many different sources, it is safe to assume that the eventual distribution of food from the General Fund was as fairly done as was humanly possible.

The handling of the supplies followed roughly the same system that the A. R. A. had used for the children's kitchen. A committee was first organized to take charge of the various products, and to be responsible for the individual receipts which were exacted from every adult. Some of the food was shipped by rail to the outlying distribution points, and the villages notified to come with their wagons and get the supplies. In other cases they were sent directly to Pokrowsk or Saratov. This was the method used by the village of Bangert, from which twenty teams came to haul away the 699 poods of provisions that had been set aside for them.

On February 25th Mr. Repp sent a detailed report to Portland, giving the names of the thirty-three villages on both the Berg and Wiesenseite to which the first Volga Relief Society food had been sent. He also included the actual division of supplies with the number of poods of lard, flour, and grits that each colony had received. After these figures, he added:

"Every person in these colonies received part of the food regardless of his need. All the supplies were divided equally and amounted to about five pounds for every man, woman and child. Within the next few days I will distri-

> bute 6000 pood more; about half of that will go into the communes on the Wiesenseite and the other half to colonies on the Bergseite."

Practically every letter written during this period mentions the slowness of the Russian transportation system. In this connection the Portland representative wrote again on March 1 to his impatient friends:

> "All Volga Relief Society funds will be used to feed adults as you subscribed and designated. Don't get excited, as we can do no more than what is being done. The railroads in this country are almost a total wreck. When I tell you that it actually took six weeks for a shipment of my supplies to go two hundred miles, you can see with what I have to contend. I am continually wiring Moscow for more food, but Russian inefficiency cannot get it to Saratov."

After his return to America, Mr. Repp told in greater detail the story of the shipment mentioned above. The food in this particular case was bound for Frank and other distant villages on the Bergseite. It was always necessary in such cases to send along armed guards to protect the supplies from possible theft. Since the distance was so great, Mr. Repp tried to be unusually careful in picking out two men who could be trusted to get the food to its destination as quickly as possible. He then waited week after week with mounting impatience for the return of the guards. When they finally did appear, they recounted the long list of difficulties that they had experienced. The engine of their train was, of course, completely outworn, and continually broke down. This necessitated repair work that often took more than a week at a time. Then when they did get started, the wood supply would run out, so that even trees along the tracks were sometimes chopped down and used for fuel. In addition, the half-starved train personnel was hostile and un-cooperative because of the empty promises of payment that they had received from the government in the past. On one occasion they even attempted to wreck the cars in a village where friends had been advised to stand ready to steal the food. It is natural to suppose that after such a tale, Mr. Repp was willing to excuse the guards, and to be thankful that the supplies had eventually reached their destination in safety.

After this first distribution of the Volga Relief Society funds in February, many letters began to arrive expressing the great gratitude of the people for the gifts sent by their American relatives. In one of these letters, dated February 27, the writer, Mr. Alexander Doell, tells us:

"During the winter months a period of horrible suffering began for the people of Wiesenmüller. The Soviet government continued to send a little help, but hundreds of our neighbors became a prey of the fam.ne. Then suddenly on February 19th the unexpected news came that adults as well as children were now to receive aid. This message came from Mr. Repp who sent an order for 300 pood of supplies to be divided equally among all living people in the village. The only way to describe our feelings is to say that if a man were sentenced to death and suddenly pardoned, he would probably experience what we felt on that day.

"To be sure, our need is still very great. But Mr. Repp has given us new courage with the assurance that this is only the first shipment of supplies and that more will follow in the future. It is impossible for us to repay you for what you have done, but we will pray to God that He continue to protect and bless your land as well as all the generous citizens who live there."

One of the villages which always seemed unusually grateful for the food which it received, was Brunnental on the Wiesenseite of the river. On one occasion in July, seventy-five separate letters of thanks were mailed in a package to the Volga Relief Society, and during the first week of March, seventeen messages were sent. At the same time Rev. J. Grasmück, the pastor of the local church, wrote to Mr. Repp:

"The help which you recently sent to our village could not have come at a more opportune time. In just another week hundreds of additional people would have died of starvation. How the sunken eyes of the people shone when I told them that I had received an order of 360 pood of supplies which we were to get at Pokrowsk. I begged the wealthier inhabitants of the village to share their remaining morsels with their more unfortunate neighbors, some of whom had had nothing to eat for several days. In this way nobody would starve in the few intervening days before the food arrived. I, myself, tried to set an example by carrying part of my meagre provisions to the houses of my poorest parishoners. After the food came, it was divided by the members of the church council to the satisfaction of the entire village."

Mr. Repp had stated in his letter of February 26th that he had an additional 60,000 pood of supplies to divide among the Volga German people. Part of this allotment went to the Wiesenseite villages of Friedenberg, Gnadentau, Morgentau, and Blumenfeld, each of which received 240 pood of products. In his letter of gratitude Rev. J. Koseiol, the pastor, mentioned that his parisioners were especially happy that these supplies had arrived before the spring rains made the roads impassable. He then adds, "With tears of joy many a father and mother carried their little sacks of flour and bowls of lard and grits home, and then thanked God on their knees that they could finally eat a decent meal again."

Another village that expressed great gratitude for its gifts from the Volga Relief Society was Kosakenstadt, or Pokrowsk, which lies on the east bank of the Volga near Saratov. The chairman of the church council, John Lick, gave the following details of the distribution of the supplies in a letter to Mr. Repp dated April 3, 1922:

"Enclosed you will find 710 receipts from the various families in Kosakenstadt who were given food from the warehouse in our town. Your instructions regarding its distribution were carried out in the following manner:

1. We carefully checked the registration statistics that had been collected by Mr. Russell Cobb, and then gave every legal member of the colony an order for food stamped with the church seal and signed by the chairman of the church council.

2. It was announced in our church that after eight oclock on the morning of March 26th the supplies would be distributed. The next morning bright and early, large throngs gathered before the designated building, and throughout the entire day, and long into the night, the work went on with the greatest speed. On the next day, March 27th, the same process was continued.

"In order to avoid all possible mistakes, every individual had to appear before a committee and show his church pass. His name was then checked with the registration statistics, and scratched off this list. Following this, the pass was stamped once more and the recipient of the food had to sign his name to a receipt. Next he was given an order to go to the granary and receive his products. In this way the work progressed with perfect order in spite of the bad weather which we had that day; and everyone got his share of the supplies, carefully weighed out down to the smallest solotnik.

The Volga Relief Society food which was distributed in February and March truly came as a Godsend to the German people, and as Rev. Koseiol had stated, it was especially important that it be distributed at this particular time. Immediately afterward the spring thaws came and made transportation by wagon almost impossible. A letter from Mr. Repp dated April 18 told that he had received no mail during the previous four weeks because of the bad roads, and Rev. Wacker wrote on April 4th, "We are cut off from the entire world. All the valleys and hollow places are so deeply filled with water that I was even unable to drive to Huck last Sunday."

In addition to the difficulties caused by the thaw and rains, the railroads were still unable to carry away all of the large quantities of supplies that had arrived in the seaport towns. Mr. Henry Ehlers, a beloved evangelist in Dinkel, realized that some Americans were unjustifiably criticizing the A. R. A. for this delay. In an attempt to clarify the situation he wrote to his friends in the United States:

> "You must remember that it is a very simple matter to send food from the United States to Riga, but from Riga to Saratov is an entirely different story. Your representatives are just as impatient as we over this delay. Fourteen days ago I asked Mr. Repp if no additional food had been designated for our village. He answered, 'Yes, the designations are here, but we haven't any products. I've already telegraphed twice to Moscow, but haven't received an answer.' Here in Russia we can understand this situation very well, but you Americans are too much inclined to judge distances in comparison with your own country, and you forget that we've had nearly eight years of war with all its resulting destruction and confusion. You may believe me when I say that in spite of all these difficulties, your representatives are doing their duty to the very best of their ability."

During the month of April, the suffering of the German-Russia people again became desperately acute. The five pounds of food which they had received from the Volga Relief Society, had long since disappeared, and in many of the villages the children's kitchens had to either close down completely or go on half-rations. Rev. Eichhorn of Messer wrote at this time that a deathly silence lay over his entire village. The inhabitants lacked the strength to even cross the streets. The only sound to disturb the ghostly solitude was the ringing of the church bells as another corpse was carried to the cemetery. In the three months since New Year both Messer and Moor had lost an additional 380 people, and in Kutter about 125 had died. These dead bodies lay unburied in a frozen condition all during the winter months and created a serious health problem with the coming of spring. Because of the great danger of a plague, which might result, the Soviet authorities did their utmost to see that graves were dug, and that decent burials finally occurred.

Throughout these months prices continued to reach unheard-of heights. A cow, which had sold for 3,000,-000 rubles in January, was worth 60 to 70,000,000 rubles in April; a pound of black bread had now increased from 14,000 to 260,000 rubles; one pound of butter cost 50,000 rubles; a box of matches, 8,000,000 rubles, etc.

However, in spite of the ever-present figures of starvation and pestilence, the warm spring air awakened a hope for life in the hearts of the Volga Germans. During the cold winter months many of them had given up all thoughts of survival and had even become reconciled to what seemed an inevitable death; but now they felt a desire to resist the spectres that had hovered so long above them. The knowledge that sufficient food would soon reach their village also strengthened them in their struggle against despair. Many of them had received letters from friends and relatives telling of the purchase of Food Drafts; they had also been promised additional supplies from the Volga Relief Society funds, and best of all was the rumor that the United States government had begun distributing millions of dollars worth of corn and seed grain.

The days slowly went by, and finally on April 18th Mr. Repp received the welcome news that food was on hand for both the children and the adults. He immediately left for Saratov where he loaded the steamer and barge for Schilling that Mr. Knies described in a previous chapter. At the same time plans were made for the allocation of the remaining Volga Relief Society food. This amounted to about 100,000 pood and was distributed during the next five weeks.

In February the only supplies that could be purchased were flour, lard and grits. But a greater variety of provisions were now on hand, so that a village received the following articles for $1,000.00 of Volga Relief Society money:

Cocoa	10	pood
Sugar	39	pood 13 pounds.
Cases of milk	68	(48 cans in case)
Flour	249	pood 9 pounds.
Beans	25	pood.
Rice	49	pood.
Lard	21	pood.
Cornmeal	60	pood. (6).

By the end of May approximately $170,000.00 worth of food had been divided among the German-Russian colonies on the two sides of the river. This was done, for the most part, by means of a special steamboat carrying 30,000 pood at a time. Four trips were made up and down the river, and the supplies were unloaded at Schilling, Dobrinka, and Bannowka on the Bergseite; and Seelmann, Kukkus and Pokrowska on the Wiesenseite. The table below shows the amount of money designated for each colony by the Volga Relief Society as well as by other organizations such as the one in Lincoln, Neb. We can also see how much was alloted by Mr. Repp out of the General Fund. These statistics include what was spent in February and March.

BERGSEITE

	V. R. S.	From Other Places	V. R. S. Gen. Fund	Total
Awilowa	$ 80.00	185.00	235.00	500.00
Alexandertal	110.00	20.00	370.00	500.00
Anton	30.00	330.00	1640.00	2000.00
Bauer	550.00	307.00	143.00	1000.00
Beideck	660.00	1820.00	520.00	3000.00
Balzer	150.00	1080.00	2770.00	4000.00
Degott			500.00	500.00
Dreispitz	70.00	70.00	360.00	500.00
Dietel	1270.00	692.00	538.00	2500.00
Doennhof	260.00	745.00	995.00	2000.00
Dobrinka	250.00	340.00	410.00	1000.00

Erlenbach	30.00	10.00	190.00	500.00
Frank	3750.00	4641.00	1609.00	10000.00
Franzosen	300.00	107.00	593.00	1000.00
Franker Kutter	360.00	1123.00	517.00	2000.00
Galka	730.00	....	270.00	1000.00
Grimm	1960.00	177.00	863.00	3000.00
Hussenbach	700.00	147.00	653.00	1500.00
Holstein	410.00	....	590.00	1000.00
Huck	1800.00	328.00	872.00	3000.00
Kraft	1250.00	200.00	550.00	2000.00
Kolb	1450.00	976.00	574.00	3000.00
Kauz	250.00	45.00	205.00	500.00
Kutter	590.00	64.00	846.00	1500.00
Kamyschin	50.00	....	450.00	500.00
Kratzke	10.00	10.00	480.00	500.00
Merkel	50.00	30.00	420.00	500.00
Mueller	130.00	10.00	360.00	500.00
Messer	810.00	257.00	933.00	2000.00
Moor	10.00	55.00	935.00	1000.00
Neu Balzer	20.00	10.00	470.00	500.00
Neu Messer	360.00	128.00	512.00	1000.00
Neu Doennhof	230.00	40.00	730.00	1000.00
Neu Norka	70.00	....	430.00	500.00
Norka	12600.00	2383.00	17.00	15000.00
Oberdorf	10.00	98.00	392.00	500.00
Pfeifer	10.00	....	490.00	500.00
Rosenberg (Umet)	190.00	655.00	155.00	1000.00
Schilling	90.00	1731.00	679.00	2500.00
Semjonowka	230.00	....	270.00	500.00
Stephan	170.00	15.00	315.00	500.00
Schwab	10.00	....	490.00	500.00
Tscherbakowka	110.00	145.00	245.00	500.00
Unterdorf	410.00	20.00	70.00	500.00
Walter	1160.00	760.00	580.00	2500.00
Walter Kutter	650.00	440.00	410.00	1500.00

WIESENSEITE

Bangert	1240.00	552.00	708.00	2500.00
Brunnental	1120.00	465.00	915.00	2500.00
Blumenfeld	....	10.00	490.00	500.00
Dinkel	1940.00	1505.00	555.00	4000.00
Eckheim	....	....	500.00	500.00
Friedenfeld	120.00	40.00	340.00	500.00
Friedenberg	....	50.00	450.00	500.00
Gnadentau	30.00	....	470.00	500.00
Hoffental	70.00	....	430.00	500.00
Hoelzel	20.00	....	480.00	500.00
Hussenbach (Gaschon)	245.00	....	255.00	500.00
Katharinental	40.00	25.00	435.00	500.00
Kukkus	2210.00	2257.00	533.00	5000.00
Konstantinowka	20.00	....	480.00	500.00
Krasny Kut	....	....	500.00	500.00
Laub	1440.00	580.00	980.00	3000.00
Laube	1420.00	553.00	1027.00	3000.00
Langenfeld	10.00	....	490.00	500.00
Liebental	10.00	....	490.00	500.00
Morgentau	170.00	....	330.00	500.00
Neu Moor	80.00	....	420.00	500.00
Neu Laub	100.00	....	400.00	500.00
Neu Bauer	130.00	....	370.00	500.00
Neu Beideck	60.00	....	440.00	500.00
Neu Schilling	430.00	....	70.00	500.00
Neu Norka	75.00	215.00	210.00	500.00
Neu Warenburg	....	....	500.00	500.00
Straub	2890.00	500.00	1110.00	4500.00
Stahl	4830.00	2099.00	571.00	7500.00
Schoental	130.00	....	370.00	500.00
Schoenfeld	60.00	....	440.00	500.00

Schoendorf	10.00	....	490.00	500.00
Strassendorf	....	60.00	440.00	500.00
Warenburg	2820.00	1089.00	1091.00	5000.00
Wiesenmueller	230.00	235.00	535.00	1000.00
Weizenfeld	....	....	500.00	500.00
Yost	1290.00	1080.00	630.00	3000.00
Aerenfeld	....	....	500.00	500.00
Kano	....	....	500.00	500.00

Another group of colonies which lie north of Saratov in the Marxstadt district received their allocations a few weeks later.

BERGSEITE

	V. R. S.	From Other Places	V. R. S. Gen. Fund	Total
Jagodnaja	1850.00	15.00	635.00	2500.00
Neu Straub	470.00	....	530.00	1000.00
Pobotschnaja	170.00	....	830.00	1000.00
Saratov	310.00	20.00	670.00	1000.00

WIESENSEITE

Alexanderhöh	....	510.00	290.00	800.00
Balakowo	30.00	....	470.00	500.00
Bohn	10.00	....	490.00	500.00
Fresental	5.00	....	500.00	505.00
Fischer	220.00	....	280.00	500.00
Gnadendorf	460.00	500.00	540.00	1500.00
Kratz	50.00	....	450.00	500.00
Kosakenstadt	100.00	....	900.00	1000.00
Krasny Jar	80.00	....	420.00	500.00
Orlowskaja	90.00	....	410.00	500.00
Rosenheim	....	18.00	482.00	500.00
Reinwald	450.00	13.00	337.00	800.00
Reinhard	10.00	10.00	480.00	500.00
Schulz	100.00	....	400.00	500.00
Schaffhausen	100.00	....	400.00	500.00
Schwed	....	50.00	450.00	500.00
Urbach	30.00	....	470.00	500.00
Marxstadt	....	....	500.00	500.00
Liilenfeld	30.00	....	470.00	500.00

In examining these statistics we note that $191,-758.13 was distributed between February 1 and July 17, the date of Mr. Repp's departure from Russia. Of this sum approximately $61,000.00 had been designated for the Bergseite, $42,000.00 for the Wiesenseite, and $88,000.00 for the General Fund. Since the amount assigned to the east side was not as large as that for the west side, the former colonies received a relatively larger share of the money from the General Fund. For example, the only colony on the Bergseite which was given assistance without having received an American contribution was the little Catholic village of Degott. On the Wiesenseite, however, the communities of Eckheim, Krasny Kut, Neu Warenburg, Weizenfeld, Aehrenfeld, Kano, and Marxstadt were all given supplies solely out of the unrestricted contributions.

It is also interesting to note that the largest specific contributions had been given by American Volga Germans to the following colonies:

Norka	$14,983.00	Warenburg	3,909.00
Frank	8,391.00	Dinkel	3,445.00
Stahl	6,929.00	Straub	3,390.00
Kukkus	4,467.00		

Since the people from Norka had shown such unusual generosity in their donations to the mother colony, Mr. Repp gave them the smallest allocation from the General Fund—only $17.00. On the other hand, more than $1000.00 was added to what had been designated for Anton, Balzer, Frank, Laube, Straub, and Warenburg, all of whom were large villages in need of additional help.

Out of the total number of 190 German colonies situated in the Saratov area, 108 received food from the funds raised by the Volga Relief Societies. The smallest sum given to any community was $500.00 and the largest amount was $15,000.00. These villages were distributed on both sides of the river in such a way that fifty lay on the Bergseite and fifty-eight on the Wiesenseite.

Mr. Repp was assisted in the distribution of Volga Relief Society money by Rev. Jacob Wagner, who had been sent from Lincoln, Nebraska, by the Central States Volga Relief Society. (7). Rev. Wagner arrived in Saratov on February 8th and made frequent trips down the Volga and through the colonies. While in Russia he visited many different families, and his long letters and reports on conditions in the villages were read with much interest by his American friends. Mr. Repp left Saratov for the United States on July 17 and during the succeeding three months Rev. Wagner allocated the money which continued to arrive for the German colonies.

The second group of letters thanking the Volga Relief Society for its gifts was quite different in tone from the ones that had been sent in February and

March. At that time there was still great danger of future starvation, but after the first of May the crisis had passed for everyone. The feeling of optimism which the German-Russians now felt is reflected in a report from the church council of Kukkus, which reads:

"On May 25 Mr. Repp arrived at Kukkus with a barge steamer carrying 24,000 pood of provisions for twelve villages, of which Kukkus alone received 3,000 pood. The ship stopped beyond the shallow water, and all products had to be brought to the shore by means of little boats. The activity out in the harbor was something which none of us had seen for a long time. Most of the unloading took place on Ascension Day. As a result, this holiday will always remain in the minds of our people as the day when the famine definitely ended. The 3,060 pood for our village was equally divided among all living souls. The task was directed by the church council who saw to it that everyone received the following supplies:

Flour	22½	pounds
Cocoa	1.63	pounds
Grits	6⅛	pounds
Lard	1⅞	pounds
Rice	3¾	pounds
Sugar	4¾	pounds
Milk (9 cans)	4¾	pounds

"These figures show that most of the families had very large loads to carry away. And what healthful nourishing food it was! Even while the gifts were being received, many of the people expressed their thanks with tears and emotion.

'It is impossible for us to ever reward you adequately, but you may rest assured that not only we, but also our children and children's children will always think of you with love and gratitude. We all realize that it was your help alone that rescued us from a certain death." (8).

Since our space is limited, it is possible to mention only two more letters of gratitude that were received at this time. The first came from Straub and was signed by the members of the church council, three of whom had the name Karle and three, Schwabenland. These men tell us:

"Last February when our distress reached its highest peak, Mr. Repp unexpectedly came and gave us an order for 30 pood of supplies. This food was brought from Pokrowsk and divided equally among all living inhabitants. We were also assured that additional supplies would soon be on hand. However, the unusually cold winter prevented the provisions from reaching us until the beginning of spring. By this time conditions were again in a terrible state, and throngs of people were dying of hunger and typhus. Then suddenly the dark night of our anguish ended. Our schoolteacher received an order to get one hundred Food Drafts that had been sent by H. P. Steitz, and J. A. Karle of Fresno, California. At the same time Mr. Repp also sent us over 4000 pood of different supplies which were again equally divided." (9).

The second message, which came from Gnadendorf and was signed by every inhabitant of the village, began with the following sentences:

"Just as little children rejoice when they receive their presents on Christmas Eve, so the village of Gnadendorf was full of happiness when we received 915 pood of supplies from America. This food was divided equally in such a way that we all were given twenty-one pounds. Since such supplies are more precious than gold, we wish to express our deepest thanks to those of you who are responsible for this gift." (10).

The Ascension Day, which was mentioned in the letter from Kukkus was also celebrated in many another village along the Volga River. In Kutter, for example, it was heralded as a day of Thanksgiving in which the children of the colony recited little poems that they had memorized. One of them may be used as a fitting conclusion for this chapter.

"Nachdem wir lange Not gelitten
Nachdem das Grab schon vor uns stand
Da kam Amerika geschritten
Mit seinen Gaben in der Hand.
Und Bruder Repp und andre mehr
    Die kamen aus der Ferne her."(11).

FOOTNOTES

1. H. H. Fisher, **op. cit.,** 413.
2. **Ibid,** 405.
3. Letter of Rev. Jacob Wagner, March 29, 1922.
4. **A. R. A. Bulletin,** Series 11, No. 43, 92.
5. Fisher, **op. cit.,** 556. In August, 1922, approximately one million adults and children were being fed daily by the A. R. A. in the Saratov area.
6. Mr. Repp's receipts. These are the products given to the village of Neu Straub.
7. A letter written by T. C. Lonergan, Executive Assistant at Moscow, on February 7, 1922, states: "Mr. Repp will handle all the business end of the Volga Relief Committee's work, such as allocation of foodstuffs . . . number of persons fed, etc.; Mr. Wagner will act as field inspector, visiting in conjunction with Mr. Repp the various communes.
8. **Volga Relief Society Bulletin,** July 29, 1922.
9. **Ibid,** August 14, 1922.
10. A letter written August 2, 1922.
11. A letter written July 13, 1922.

Chapter Seven.

CORN AND CLOTHING.

In spite of the remarkably generous contributions of the Volga Germans that were mentioned in a previous chapter, it is necessary to point out that even more money was spent on their friends and relatives by the American Relief Administration. The day-by-day feeding of the children was entirely taken care of in this way, and after the first of April the adults as well as the children were given aid.

As soon as the agreement with Litvinov was signed, Dr. Vernon Kellogg, a former relief worker in Belgium, was sent to Russia to make a personal survey of conditions for Herbert Hoover. The same task was also given to ex-governor Goodrich of Indiana, who left the United States with Mr. George Repp. Mr. Kellogg remained in Russia from September 19 to October 3, and Gov. Goodrich from October 4 to November 14. Upon returning to the United States, both men reported that the situation was even more urgent than they had expected, and that it was absolutely necessary that seed wheat and food for the adults be sent to Russia immediately.

In view of the necessity for speed, Herbert Hoover then decided to ask the American Congress for an appropriation of $20,000,000.00 with which to buy large supplies of corn and seed grain. At this time there was an immense surplus of farm products in the United States, and as he pointed out, the passage of such a measure would aid our American farmers, and also be means of salvation for millions of Russian peasants.

This proposal received the support of President Harding, who recommended it in his message to Congress on December 6, 1921. The House Committee on Foreign Affairs held a hearing on the bill on December 13 and 14. Mr. Hoover appeared at these meetings with both Dr. Kellogg and Gov. Goodrich, who were able to

give first-hand information on what they themselves
had seen. As a result of their recommendations, the
bill was reported back to the House, and after several
days of debate, was passed by Congress on December
22nd. (1).

It had been hoped that the corn would reach the
Russian peasants before the coming of the spring
thaws, and every effort was made in America to send
ships to the Black Sea as quickly as possible. However,
the lack of transportation facilities, which have so often
been mentioned, again interfered with these plans, and
it usually took until the first week of April before the
grain reached the necessary distribution points.

The first shipment for the German-Russian people
was sent by rail along the west side of the Volga, was
unloaded directly from the train at the Medwediza and
Lapschinskaja stations. Mr. Repp, who was in Balzer
at the time, sent out couriers to both the northern and
the southern villages in order to inform the Volga Germans of the arrival of the corn and of the place where
it could be obtained. Since the roads were impassable
at that time, most of these men had to travel on foot in
order to reach their destination.

One of the best descriptions of the actual unloading
of the grain and its delivery to the people is given by
John Gregg in his "General Report" of the Saratov
area. Here we are told:

> "In more fortunate areas, special trains went along the
> rickety railway lines, stopping at villages to which the
> peasants had been warned to come with their carts and
> their feeding lists. An American who supervised this, tells
> of one place where they mobilized twenty persons—all who
> could read and write in the town — and enrolled them as
> clerks to write and register orders. The local military
> force was called out to keep the people in line as they
> registered. At first, as the lines of peasants passed the
> cars, they tramped through mud, but it was soon dried up
> by the pressure of many feet. Each recipient of corn car-
> ried away a duplicate receipt bearing the inscription 'free
> American corn.' A change came over the whole community
> as the lines passed the car where the peasants received the
> corn and started in diverse directions towards their vil-
> lages. The Easter bells were ringing. One group of men
> and women, before they set out on their long march to
> their homes, sought out the American to tell him that they

DISTRIBUTING AMERICAN SEED WHEAT. STATION MEDWEDZ.

and their neighbors would thereafter always associate the ringing of Easter bells with the yellow American corn, which came at that season to rescue them from death." (2)

Mr. Repp's first mention of the corn distribution is on April 18, when he wrote:

"The American Relief Administration corn has landed. An enormous amount of this corn has gone to our German people, the Bergseite colonies alone getting 45 carloads with 1000 pood to the car. I have sent orders to all the colonies, some of which have already got their share and the balance will get their's soon."

Mr. Philip Knies in his letter of April 29 also mentions the corn and tells that the 45,000 pood had been divided in the following manner:

	Duration	Population	Pood and Pounds	
Balzer Rayon, 4 weeks after April 17		18,381	12,866	28
Franker Rayon, 6 weeks after April 17		7,825	8,213	30
Kamenkar Rayon, 6 weeks after April 10		9,400	9,860	....
Dobrinka Rayon, 8 weeks after April 10		10,266	14,372	16

Although the roads were passable by now, there was still a great deal of mud, which made it difficult for the villages along the Volga to send teams of horses or oxen to the railroad stations. However, because of the great need for food, and the knowledge that everyone above the age of fifteen would share in the distribution regardless of his relative poverty, wagons and sledges soon found their way to the various distribution centers. One of the most interesting snapshots that Mr. Repp brought back to the United States, shows hundreds of these conveyances lined up along the railroad tracks to receive the precious cargo for their villages. After the teamsters returned home, the corn was usually given out in fourteen-pound lots, which were supposed to last an individual for two weeks. At the end of that period an additional supply was distributed. The corn either came as cornmeal or else in the whole kernel. In the latter case, it had to be ground by the peasants on their primitive hand mills before being boiled into a porridge.

Since the Volga Germans had been told that the distribution of corn would continue throughout the summer months, many of them felt that there was no further necessity of putting aside a reserve for the future. For over a year, thousands of them had been haunted by the fear of starvation, and now with the promise of continued assistance, many fathers and mothers carried their bags of grain home with the mental vow, "Tonight I'm going to eat a really big meal." The A. R. A. men had been afraid of this reaction, and as the corn was taken away, would warn the people against over-eating. But in spite of all advice, the sight of such a large quantity of food was too difficult to resist, and in every village deaths occurred from over-indulgence at the first meal.

Along with the corn, large shipments of seed wheat also began to arrive in the German colonies. Part of this was bought with the money appropriated by the American Congress, but the larger share was purchased with Soviet gold that had been sent to our country by the Russian government. Approximately ten million dollars, divided in the following manner was spent on seed alone:

United States	$2,948,485.24
Soviet Gold	7,034.874.30
	$9,983,359.54

Although these figures represent what was sent to the entire Soviet Union, a letter written by Rev. Wacker on May 1 tells that his village of Norka also received its share of both the corn and the seed wheat:

"The winter snow was scarcely melted, when we had several severe rain storms, but in spite of the resulting bad roads, wagons were sent to the stations at Medwediza, which lies sixty verst away, to get our seed wheat and the American corn. This difficult journey caused the loss of some of our remaining livestock, especailly on one hot day when several oxen fell dead.

"However, as a result of these trips, the village of Norka now has sufficient seed wheat for its needs. According to a Soviet decree, the distribution depended upon the amount of livestock that is still in our possession, and since our village is more fortunate in this respect than others, we were given 25,000 pood and Huck 20,000 pood.

"For several days people have been busy plowing and sowing the grain. The greatest difficulty is caused by our lack of sufficient livestock. The horses and oxen that we do have, are in too weak a condition to be of much help, and many of the people have lost all of their animals.

"On April 17 our kitchens had to close because of a shortage of products, but the distress which such an act would ordinarily have caused was greatly diminished by the timely arrival of the American corn during Easter week. Today a notice also came that food for the children was now on hand in Schilling.

"If it had not been for the corn, many people would have starved to death and many others would not have had the strength to do their heavy spring work. Of course there is still a great need for different kinds of food. Next to the lack of wheat for bread we feel the necessity of lard and salt. The poorest people make their corn porridge without being able to add any shortening, and in many cases without salt. The government has a complete monopoly on all salt sold in the cities, but in the villages it is handled by private traders. About six weeks ago I paid 35,000 rubles for half a pood, and then it was of a very poor quality.'

In the meantime large supplies of corn were also being distributed among the Wiesenseite villages. The ice on the Volga had been gone for some time, and it was found that the quickest way of getting food to this side was to send barges down the river to the stations where the A. R. A. had located its warehouses. In this connection Mr. Repp wrote on May 18th:

"I have just spent a week on the Volga unloading five barges of corn which will be distributed on both sides of the river. This shipment amounted to over one hundred thousand pood, and was paid for by the American Relief Administration. One barge was unloaded at Kukkus, one at Seelmann, one at Schilling, one at Bannowka, and the other at N. Dobrinka. This will feed a good many people."

During the following months, the Russian transportation system became more and more dependable, so that the A. R. A. was able to rely upon a steady stream of supplies. This changed condition was caused to a great extent by the appointment of Mr. Djerjinsky as Commissar of Communications in April. The difference between Mr. Djerjinsky and his predecessor is shown in one of the first commands that he issued to a subordinate, "Don't promise a single railroad car that you cannot deliver . . . say exactly how many you can deliver and then deliver them." (4).

A second factor that improved the situation tremendously was the breaking of the ice on the Volga after March 24, so that supplies could now reach the villages

— 111 —

by means of barges and steamers. Some of the food was sent by rail to Nijni-Novgorod and from there down the Volga to Saratov 1,130 miles away. Other supplies coming from the Black Sea were transferred to boats at Tzaritzin and then moved north to Saratov. Although it may seem strange to an American, the speed of river transport was at that time immeasurably greater than rail, and for that reason was preferred by the A. R. A. men. (5).

Since more than 700,000 German and Russian adults were being fed from Saratov in the summer of 1922, it is impossible to give exact figures on the distribution of corn among the German colonies alone. However, the following stations for adult feeding in this area show a continuous rate of increase until July, and then a decided drop in October after the crisis was definitely over.

March, 1922	176	August	529,231
April	55,618	September	553,118
May	468,211	October	51,481
June	738,662	November	6,043
July	748,802	December	4,444

We have already been told that 46,000 Germans on the Bergseite received corn in April. These figures would thereafter prove that as far as the Saratov area was concerned, the largest part of the April shipment was distributed among the German-speaking people.

At the end of his discussion on the American corn, Mr. Fisher mentions that as soon as the news of its arrival reached the Russian people, thousands of panic-stricken peasants, who had fled from their villages began to return home. The A. R. A. did everything possible to aid them in this exodus, and even provided them with food for their journey. He then concludes:

"The most striking of all the changes produced by the corn was the abrupt decrease in the number of deaths from starvation throughout the famine zone. It was not necessary for American food to reach every individual to bring about this remarkable change throughout this vast territory. Almost as important as the food itself was the knowledge that it was coming in increasing quantities. The prices of local food products everywhere dropped, and such hidden supplies as existed began to be revealed. People were still underfed; there were still occasional deaths from starvation, and distress was everywhere; but, within a few weeks' time, the demand which began to be most widely expressed was not for food, but for horses, tools, and the supplies necessary for the planting season. The Russians were looking ahead." (7).

While the condition of the German-Russian people became steadily better after the first of May, this particular month had a much less pleasant connotation for Mr. Repp. All the A. R. A. men in Saratov received periodic injections against the contagious diseases which were rampant at that time. On May 27th after one of his trips down the Volga, Mr. Repp was given a shot for paratyphoid cholera, and within a few hours became seriously ill. The American doctor at the Saratov headquarters became so alarmed at his condition that a Russian physician was called in for consultation.

During the critical period in which Mr. Repp was confined to his bed, the other Americans stationed at Saratov clearly showed the esteem and affection with which they regarded him. He was once heard to express a desire for some fresh fruit, and as a result, one of the men spent an entire afternoon visiting the various market places until he was finally able to find a few shriveled oranges which he brought apologetically back with him. A little fourteen-year-old girl named Anna Lipke, whose mother was the housekeeper at the A.R.A. home, also won his gratitude by the unfailing solicitude with which she waited upon him. However, the illness did not prove fatal, and on June 14th he again accompanied a barge down the Volga. At the same time arrangements were made for the distribution of Volga Relief Society funds to the people living in the Marxstadt district. We have already heard that this completed the allocation of approximately $192,000.00 of the money contributed by the Portland and the Lincoln organizations.

Mr. Repp now felt that the task for which he had come to Russia was accomplished, and decided to leave for the United States on July 17. The knowledge that Rev. Jacob Wagner was on hand to carry on the work of the Volga Relief Societies made it easier for him to come to this conclusion.

Upon arriving in New York, where he was met by his wife, he received a telegram from the Central States Society asking him to address their organization. The courtesy and kindness which the Lincoln people showed Mr. and Mrs. Repp upon their arrival in that city were never forgotten by them. At this time they were also able to meet such outstanding local leaders as Dr. H. P. Wekesser, Mr. John Rohrig, Mr. H. J. Amen, Mr. F. A. Lorenz, etc.

A second reception was held in Portland, Oregon, on Sunday, September 24, in the Zion Congregational Church. On this occasion Mr. John W. Miller gave a summary of the work that had been done in Portland, and Mr. Repp reported on conditions in Russia.

During the succeeding weeks the Volga Relief Society received many letters from Russia telling of the fine work that had been done by their representative during his nine months in that country. One of these, which was written by Mr. Waldemar Kisselmann of Balzer, is dated July 8, and was addressed to Mrs. George Repp:

> "Your husband left Balzer today after saying good-bye to his many good friends. It is impossible for me to describe the difficulty of the task that faced him, and also his unfailing patience in handling the many problems that arose. The famine conditions were indiscribably bad in our villages, but nevertheless he always found a method of sending A. R. A. funds to the places where they were most needed. In cases of the most urgent distress, he even gave some of his own money to those families who needed it so desperately bad.

> "Many of these people have come to me in the last few days and have asked that I express to him and to you their deepest and warmest thanks for what they received. You could not possibly imagine how hopeless our situation formerly was, but because of the work of men like your husband, thousands of people have been saved from starvation. Often in the stormiest weather he would drive to distant villages where the need was greatest. No rain, no cold, no contagious disease ever held h'm back. He never relaxed. His food and rest were seldom taken at the proper time. His work always came first.

> "And so in the name of the thousands of hungry people who have been fed, I wish to thank him, and you, as well as the kindly governor of Indiana who came to our aid."

Before bringing this chapter to a close, mention should be made of one more way in which aid was sent to the Volga Germans in Russia. This was by means of two large shipments of clothing that were gathered by the officers of the Lincoln society.

In a previous chapter we learned that many members of the Portland organization had contributed boxes of new and used clothing which were sent to Russia for general distribution by the National Lutheran Council. This clothing was eventually given to German villages located in many different sections of Russia. But since the Volga Germans were particularly anxious to help their own relatives, they were very happy to hear in January, 1922, that the Soviet government had agreed to deliver eleven-pound packages to a definite recipient. (8) Nevertheless, this method was to prove a great disappointment to most of the people who took advantage of it, since they soon heard that the packages usually arrived with many of the contents stolen. Further difficulties were revealed by Rev. Wacker in a letter dated April 28, in which he said:

> "Packages of clothing recently arrived in Norka for some of our people. One of these, a Mr. Deines, came to see me last night and complained bitterly over what had happened. His friends had sent him eleven pounds of clothing, but before getting the package he was expected to pay 6,800 rubles in taxes. Since the man did not even possess such a large sum of money, the package was opened, and the largest part of the contents were taken away from him by the authorities.

> "The National Lutheran Council is distributing some used clothing, but is unable to make much of an impression in view of our great need. Only the poorest families are being helped, but even those people who were formerly considered wealthy are now lacking every kind of material."

From the Wiesenseite a similar letter came from Blumenfeld when the schoolteacher of the village wrote on March 5th:

> "A great need for clothing exists in the Volga valley. Since it is now winter, many people are still wearing clothes made out of sheepskins, but their underwear scarcely covers their bodies. Practically all shops are standing empty, and the few things that do remain cost millions of rubles. The hope has often been expressed that America

will be able to do something regarding this shortage as well."

In answer to appeals such as these, the Central States Volga Relief Society decided to send a shipment of new and used clothing directly to the German colonies and have it accompained and distributed by one of their own men. Volga Relief Societies throughout the entire United States were notified of this decision and were urged to have their contributions in Lincoln, Nebraska, by July 5th. The A. R. A. also gave its permission to the choosing of a third representative; and as a result, Mr. Jacob Volz of York, Nebraska, was nominated in a meeting held on June 12th.

The response to Dr. Wekesser's circular letter was so great that in a few weeks' time 66,303 pounds of new and used clothing were collected. (9). Practically all of the boxes were packed in Lincoln and then sent to the warehouse of the American Friends Service Committee in Philadelphia. The Central States Society had planned to ship their clothing through this organization, but at the last minute the A. R. A. agreed to transport the boxes from New York free of charge.

Mr. Volz left the United States on August 23, and arrived in Russia during the month of September. Rev. Jacob Wagner was still in Saratov at the time, but after making a tour through the colonies with his successor, he left for America in October. The bales of clothing reached Saratov on October 17, and were distributed by Mr. Volz from a warehouse at Schilling. All of the boxes had been marked for specific colonies, and the delivery was made according to instructions.

The appreciation expressed by the Volga Germans for this clothing was so great that a second circular letter was sent from Lincoln on December 8 telling that another shipment would be forwarded in February. This consignment consisted of 64,757 pounds (10), and contained $2000.00 of new material purchased with relief society funds. (11).

A great deal of praise should be given to the Lincoln organization for the long hours of labor connected with the packing and shipping of these two large consign-

ments of clothing. Mention should also be made of Mr.
J. J. Stroh, who accompanied the first shipment to
Philadelphia; of Mr. John Rohrig and Mr. Adolf Lebsock, whose buildings were used for storage and packing purposes, and of the Ladies Aids in the various
churches who assisted with the work. But perhaps the
greatest credit of all belongs to Dr. H. P. Wekesser, the
outstanding president of the society, who first conceiv-
ed this plan of sending direct aid to the Volga colonies.

Just as with the previous shipment, the A. R. A.
agreed to pay all transportation costs of the clothing
from New York to Saratov, and on May 19 Mr. Volz *1923*
was able to send a welcome cable telling that the second
consignment had also arrived safely, and would be distributed in the designated villages.

It should be pointed out that Mr. Volz not only took
charge of these two shipments, but also allocated approximately $10,000.00 in Food and Clothing Drafts, as
well as other supplies bought with money that had been
sent directly to him for the poorest people of the villages. (12). In addition, he took an active interest in
the A.R. A. kitchens which had closed in the early fall
but re-opened for the most needy children in November. During the entire period of nine months that he
remained in Russia, Mr. Volz showed such unusual en-
ergy and good spirits that his departure on June 15,
1923, was regretted by many friends.

In the meantime the A. R. A. had signed an agreement with the Soviet Union on October 26, 1922, according to which a Clothing Draft system was inaugu-
rated. These remittances were sold after November 15
with the definite understanding that no deliveries
would be guaranteed until the middle of January. As
soon as the agreement was made, over one million yards
of textiles, including muslin, flannel, and lining were
sent to Russia for the make-up of the packages. Each
draft sold for $20.00 and entitled the recipient to re-
ceive:

4½ yards 54-in. all-wool cloth, sufficient to make one suit of clothes for either man or woman or for two children's outer garments.

8 yards flannelette, sufficient for either two men's shirts or two women's shirtwaists.

4 yards lining.

16 yards muslin, sufficient for four suits of underclothing.

8 large black ivory buttons.

16 small black ivory buttons.

24 small white bone buttons.

2 spools each of black and white thread. (13).

These Clothing Drafts never proved as popular as the Food Drafts had been. During the winter of 1921-1922, Mrs. Repp had often sold $1500.00 worth of remittances in one week, but in a letter written by her husband to John Gregg on January 15, he mentioned that she was now averaging only $100.00.

The sale of both the Clothing and Food Drafts was discontinued by the A.R.A. on March 15, 1923. At that time it was reported that they had distributed $9,305,300.00 in Food Remittances throughout the entire Soviet Union, and $737,317.12 in Clothing Remittances.

Two months later Lincoln Hutchinson made a careful survey of economic conditions in Russia, and as a result of his findings, the A. R. A. decided that its presence was no longer necessary. A liquidation agreement with the Soviet Union was signed on June 15, and by July 4, 1923, after the "inevitable festivities", the last district headquarters had closed its doors, and the relief personnel was on its way home. (14).

However, even before the A. R. A. left Russia, the Volga Relief Society in Portland, Oregon, was officially dissolved as an independent organization. This was done on November 4, 1922, during a National Convention of all Volga Germans, which was held in Lincoln, Nebraska. At that time the Portland, Lincoln, and Colorado societies consolidated into a united body called the American Volga Relief Society. During the four years that it remained in existence, the leadership of the organization was carried on for the most part by the men in Lincoln. Dr. H. P. Wekesser was chosen president at the first convention, but because of his untimely death on December 15, 1922, the work was carried on by the first vice-president, Mr. John Rohrig. In the following year Mr. H. J. Amen was elected president.

On December 12, 1922, Mr. Miller mailed his last circular letter to the many branches that had co-operated so faithfully with him. He explained that the headquarters of the new organization were now in Lincoln, and urged all members of the Volga Relief Society to give Dr. Wekesser and the other officials the same splendid support that they had formerly given him. In the same letter he included a complete financial report on all the money that had been sent to Portland.

At that time it was thought that relief work could continue indefinitely in the German colonies, but after the A. R. A. left Russia, the Volga Germans in America found it increasingly difficult to send help to their relatives across the seas. However, one more outstanding task was performed when Rev. Kuehne of Lincoln left for Germany on December 6, 1923, with 21,700 pounds of clothing consigned to the German Red Cross in Berlin. (15). Some of this clothing was given to Volga German refugees who had fled from their native villages and were now living in large camps at Bielefeld, Frankfurt on the Oder, Zossen, etc. In addition to the clothing, the American Volga Relief Society also sent two carloads of food such as beans, rice, flour, and dried fruits for distribution by Rev. Kuehne.

During the four years of its existence, the society had annual conventions which took place in the following cities:

Greeley, Colorado, August 22-23, 1923.
Portland, Oregon, June 11-15, 1924.
Fresno, California, September 30 - October 4, 1925.
Lincoln, Nebraska, June 23-27, 1926.

The last convention was of unusual interest because on Sunday afternoon of June 27, a special program was held in Sutton, Nebraska, honoring the coming of the first Volga pioneers to the United States. Although very little relief work could be done during these years, the conventions were of great value in renewing friendships and in keeping Volga Germans throughout the entire United States in contact with each other.

REFERENCES.

1. H. H. Fisher, **op. cit.,** 143-151.
2. **Ibid,** 223.
3. Surface and Bland, **American Food in the World and Reconstruction Period,** 255.
4. **A. R. A. Bulletin,** Series 2, No. 42, 55.
5. **Ibid,** 74-77.
6. H. H. Fisher, **op. cit.,** 556.
7. **Ibid,** 226-227.
8. **Volga Relief Society Bulletin,** January 26, 1922.
9. G. J. Schmidt, **op. cit.,** 5.
10. **Ibid,** 6.
11. **Minute Book of the American Volga Relief Society,** Jan. 19, 1923.
12. **Ibid.** Mr. Volz was actually sent $11,000.00, but part of it arrived too late for delivery and was returned to Lincoln, Nebraska, by the A. R. A. in October, 1923. The money was sent in the following manner:

    December 27—$2000.00 Clothing Drafts.
    January 8—$2000.00 Food Drafts.
    January 22—$3000.00 General Supplies.
    March 5—$1000.00 Food Drafts.
    April 16—$1000.00 General Supplies.
    May 21—$1000.00 Clothing and other supplies. (Part of this was returned.
    May 28—$1000.00 Cash. (This was all returned.)
13. Included in a letter from Dr. H. P. Wekesser to all the branches November 24, 1922. Also in an **A. R. A. Bulletin,** Jan. 25, 1923.
14. Surface-Bland, **op. cit.,** 264.
15. Mentioned in a letter sent to Portland by Mr. H. J. Amen on November 22, 1923. Four additional boxes were sent to New York by the Portland society.

Chapter Eight.

CONCLUSION.

In writing a final summary of the work done by the Volga Relief Society from August 11, 1921 to November 4, 1922, there are several predominating factors which should be mentioned.

The first is the fine spirit of co-operation between the Portland society and the A. R. A. in New York. Mr. Hoover's organization already had such a world-wide reputation because of the splendid work that it had done in Belgium, France, and Central Europe, that the officials of the Volga Relief Society always felt the utmost confidence in the organization through which they were distributing their money. They realized how difficult it would be to send adequate help to their relatives by means of privately shipped food packages, and consequently were very happy to be able to work through the medium of so reliable an organization as the A. R. A. In addition, they always welcomed any suggestions from the officials in New York, and followed such suggestions as closely as possible.

Since the thought uppermost in the officers' minds was to get help to their relatives as speedily as possible, they wasted no time in an unnecessary investigation of the American Relief Administration, but simply collected their money, chose a representative, and sent him to Russia — all within a period of approximately four weeks' time. The wisdom of their methods is shown by the fact that Mr. Repp was able to arrive in Saratov several months earlier than the representative of any other charitable organization. (1).

It was also very fortunate for the society that Governor Goodrich happened to leave for Russia on the same boat with Mr. Repp, and that after his arrival in Saratov he made a personal survey of the German communes. The sympathetic report on the people living in the colonies, which he brought back to America with him, undoubtedly influenced the A. R. A. to take a much greater interest in the Volga Germans than would otherwise have been the case.

Many of the letters sent from the New York office during the winter of 1921-1922 refer to the unusual efficiency with which the Portland relief society was organized. On January 27, for example, Mr. Page wrote to the "California Post":

> "We should like to point out that all of this work that is being done in the German communes is primarily due to the efficiency, courtesy and co-operation which we have received from Mr. Miller and the various state Volga Relief Societies. We personally consider that the Volga German-Russians in this country and the Germans in the Volga communes owe a very great debt of gratitude to the organizers of the Volga Relief Society in Portland and of its various branches."

In telling that the famine was completely broken with the distribution of the corn and seed grain, Mr. Page again wrote on May 26th:

> "I think this ought to be good news to your people, who have so generously contributed of their resources, not only to keep life in their countrymen, but what is perhaps more important, to give hope to them ... You may rest assured that not only have no other communities of Germans equalled the efforts of the Volga Relief Society due practically entirely to the activities of your Portland organization, but no other organization outside, of course, of the various members of the European Relief Council, of any race or religion has equalled yours. It's a great job!"

The second outstanding factor in the history of the Volga Relief Society was the confidence that so many Volga Germans in America had in the Portland organization. It was perhaps natural for this to be true of the people who were personally acquainted with the officers, but one cannot help but be impressed by the fact that total strangers in one hundred and one communities of the United States, Canada, and South America, sent their money to Portland. It is needless to say that without the help of these outside branches, the Volga Relief Society could never have accomplished what it did.

One explanation for the extraordinary response to Mr. Miller's circulars, was perhaps the fact that the first letters were sent to the pastors of churches with a German-Russian membership. This act in itself may have helped to create confidence. But the chief reason was undoubtedly the burning desire of many Volga Germans to help their unfortunate relatives across the ocean. The speed with which they began organizing branch societies would at least indicate that the wish to help was in their hearts even before Mr. Miller's letters came.

It is naturally impossible to tell in detail the story of all the branches and to mention by name the many officers who so graciously gave their time and effort in behalf of the societies. Every check sent to Portland meant that somebody had to take charge of the work of raising and forwarding the money. A great deal of correspondence was also carried on with either the Volga Relief Society officials or with the men in the A. R. A. office. And in addition, these branch officers usually assisted in filling out the thousands of Food Drafts that were sent to Russia. Many of the men in both the Portland and the Lincoln societies who carried the heaviest burden of this work during the years 1921-1923 are no longer living, but their children can always remember with pride the important part which they took in carrying out this great task.

More specific credit should also be given to the ministers of the many Volga German churches in the United States. The reader has undoubtedly noticed how often the pastor of the community served as the president or as secretary of the organization. Religion has always been an important factor in the life of the Volga Germans, and it was natural that in a crisis like this, they should turn to their ministers for assistance. The success of the Volga Relief Society can be credited to a great extent to these pastors who so often assumed the responsibility of seeing that branch societies were organized.

But in the final analysis, the greatest honor goes to the thousands of nameless Volga German men and women who actually contributed the money that was sent across the seas. Their donations often came out of painfully-earned savings, and in many cases represented a great financial sacrifice. Nevertheless, the funds were always given in an unhesitating manner, and with the single hope that they reach the designated recipient or village before it was too late. The achievements of every branch of the Volga Relief Society were so remarkable, that it is difficult to pick out individual communities for special reference. Nevertheless, the following examples of unusual generosity cannot be overlooked.

The little town of Odessa, Washington, has a population of approximately 800 people, with about half of its German-Russian citizens coming from the Black Sea area and the other half from the Volga. Both of these groups responded with such zeal that they succeeded in raising $4184.84 for General Feeding in the colonies. This contribution represents the largest sum raised by any small town connected with the Volga Relief Society. In fact, it was only surpassed by the three cities of Portland, Fresno, and Denver. A great deal of the credit for this remarkable achievement should go to the capable officers of the society, and particularly its president, Rev. J. V. G. Smith and the secretary-treasurer, Rev. J. G. Eckhardt.

The organization of the branches in Nebraska, Colorado, and Montana was mentioned in connection with Rev. Henry Hagelganz's visit to those states. Because of the large number of Volga Germans located in Denver, it was logical that that city should contribute the most money. However, one of the most unusual incidents is connected with the society at Fort Morgan. After the Food Draft system was introduced, the majority of the Volga Germans in America naturally preferred to send money directly to their own relatives, rather than to Portland for General Feeding. In spite of this fact the people of Fort Morgan sent one thousand dollars to Mr. Miller on April 22. 1922. five months after the Food Drafts had been introduced. More than half of this amount was not specified for definite villages, but instead was put into the General Fund for the colonies that were in greatest need of aid.

The story of what happened in Canada should also be included. A large part of the Volga Germans in that country had just suffered several severe crop failures, and could not have been expected to give as generously as those in the United States. Many of them were in actual need themselves. But in spite of their own poverty, they were willing to assist their more unfortunate relatives in Russia. Rev. Theo. Strobel of Leader, Sask., wrote in this connection on June 6, 1922:

> "Our Canadian people have not contributed as much money as did the American people, but when one considers their condition, it is easy to realize that they have done all they could. Many of them have borrowed money for this cause. Others, I know, are walking to church, leaving their cars unused, in order to save a little money for their starving relatives."

After reading letters such as these, the sum of $3,-677.85, which was sent from the Canadian towns, takes on an added significance. As far as the large cities are concerned, one notices that Fresno, California, and Portland, Oregon, contributed most generously to the Volga Relief Society. According to Richard Sallet there were 8000 Protestant Volga Germans living in California in the year 1920, and 3750 in Oregon. When one considers that Fresno contributed more than $37,000.00 for General Feeding, and possibly an equal sum in Food Drafts, the amount of money given per capita becomes amazingly high.

The record of the smaller Portland society in raising $58,766.86 for General Feeding and Food Drafts is even more outstanding — when considered on a per capita basis. In many cases single individuals contributed $500.00 for General Feeding, and then sent additional monthly Food Drafts to all their relatives. Many of the Portland people, just as those in other communities, were far from wealthy, and consequently, the pledging of such liberal sums represented a very great sacrifice. (2).

There are two other ways in which the Volga Relief Society was an unusual organization. The first is that practically every cent of the money raised for relief purposes came from the members of the society itself, and not from other groups of Americans. There are only a few minor exceptions to this general rule. In a letter dated November 8, 1922, Rev. Schmalle of Fresno mentioned a "Tag Day" that would take place in his city on the following Saturday. Approximately $600.00 was raised by the Fresno society in this manner. In May, 1922, Rev. Hergert of Fort Collins, Colo., also tells of a "Drive" that resulted in the acquisition of $341.61. However, the amount of money raised in this manner is so insignificant when compared to what was given by the Volga Germans themselves that it would be safe to say that at least 98 per cent of all the contributions were pledged in the regular meetings by the members of the society.

The second outstanding characteristic of the Volga Relief Society is the economy with which the organization was conducted. Small running expenses, such as the purchase of stamps, paper, and the printing of circular letters were paid by means of a free-will offering taken in the weekly meetings. But neither Mr. Miller who wrote the many circular letters that were sent to all the branches, or Mrs. George Repp, whose home was used as an office to which hundreds of people came every month, were ever paid for the enormous amount of work that they did. The largest part of Mr. Miller's tasks had to be done in the evening after he left his own office, and during the winter months of 1921-1922 he and Mrs. Repp spent practically every night going over their correspondence and making plans for the development of the societies. As a result of the outstanding services of these and the other officers, every cent of money designated for relief went for that definite purpose.

The Volga Relief Society was also unusually fortunate in having Mr. Repp as its representative in Russia. Because of the fact that he was accepted as a member of the A. R. A. staff, it was not necessary for the society to pay for any of his expenses during the nine months that he remained in the Soviet Union. This meant that the money which the Portland people would have otherwise spent for this purpose could all be contributed to the General Feeding Fund.

The fact that the A. R. A. held Mr. Repp's services in high esteem is shown by the appreciative statements that were sent to Portland by John Ellingston of the Moscow Historical Division, John Gregg of Saratov, Mr. Frank Page of New York and Mr. Walter Lyman Brown in London. In Mr. Fisher's book we read, "Repp's tact, singleness of purpose, and great ability were responsible for the establishment of the work in the colonies on a firm foundation which insured the success of the relief in these regions." (3).

On September 14, 1922, Mr. Herbert Hoover also wrote:

> "The German-Russian people both in this country and along the Volga owe you a great debt of gratitude. The American Relief Administration realizes this perhaps more than your own people do, for we have seen the efficiency and devotion displayed in your work at first hand. I should like to express to you both in the name of the A. R. A. and myself, personally, our hearty appreciation and thanks."

However, it should be pointed out, that if it had not been for the help of the American Relief Administration, the philanthropy of the Volga German people and the capable work of their representatives would have been of much less benefit to their friends and relatives. During the twenty-two months that the A. R. A. remained in Russia it distributed $61,500,000.00 in food, clothing, and medicine, which constituted ninety per cent of all the foreign aid given to the Soviet Union during those years. (4). The German colonies received their share of this amount in the form of clothing and food for the children, corn for the adult population, seed wheat for their fields, and medical supplies for their hospitals. All of this was done in addition to what was sent by American friends in the form of Food Drafts, Clothing, and Volga Relief Society funds.

It should also be pointed out that because of the agreement with Litvinov, all American products were given free transportation across Russia by the Soviet government, and in spite of the delays, reached their destination much faster than privately shipped goods.

It is easy to imagine the difficulties which would have faced the Volga Relief Society, if it had attempted to handle its funds independently of the New York office. Another important point is that since Mr. Repp purchased his supplies from the A. R. A. at Saratov, it was possible for him to buy his food at a tremendous saving, since no transportation cost was included.

Credit should also be given to the efficiency, courage and devotion to duty that was shown by the A.R.A. officials and field workers in the Saratov area. The names of John Gregg, Russell Cobb, and Paul Clapp have already been mentioned, but there were at least thirteen other Americans who took part in the work of this region. Many of their tasks consisted of the writing of lengthy statistical reports, checking the arrival of the freight cars, supervising the loading of barges, etc. Their work was often done under extraordinary difficulties, and in unhealthy surroundings, but they always succeeded in carrying out their undertaking in a tireless and resourceful manner. As a foreign observer once remarked, "The A. R. A. has accomplished 95 per cent of what it set out to do, 125 per cent of what was possible." (5).

In his book, "I Write as I Please", Walter Duranty testified to the high calibre of the A. R. A. men when he said:

"Many harsh things have been said about Mr. Hoover . . but I take off my hat with a low bow to his Relief Administration. From every point of view they were a splendid set of men, efficient, honest, friendly and intensely loyal to each other and to 'The Chief' as they called him . . . From its start in Belgium in the winter of 1914-1915 to its finish in Moscow in the summer of 1923, the A. R. A. did its job often in circumstances of great delicacy, difficulty, and actual danger, with a maximum of success and a minimum of cost." (6).

It was later a matter of great regret to the Volga Germans in America that the wonderful work accomplished in Russia between 1921-1922 could not prevent future years of poverty and distress from coming to their relatives. But in spite of this fact, the story of the American Relief Administration will always stand as an enduring monument to the disinterested friendship and generosity of the United States, just as the history of the Volga Relief Society reflects the loyalty and love of the many people who helped in its creation.

FOOTNOTES

1. Mr. Gustav F. Beschorner and Dr. Albert C. Ernst, representatives of the National Lutheran Council arrived in February, 1922.

2. Since funds were sent by the Volga Germans to other organizations, such as the National Lutheran Council, it is difficult to make comparisons of the total sums contributed by a specific community. According to Richard Sallet, op. cit., 47, Chicago, Illinois, has more Volga Germans than any other city in the United States, but the three cities of Fresno, Portland, and Lincoln, contributed a great deal more money to the Volga Relief Societies.

3. H. H. Fisher, op. cit., 467.

4. The figure of $61,500,000.00 is given by H. H. Fisher, op. cit., 553. The statement that the United States gave 90 per cent of all foreign aid is mentioned in a letter written by Frank Page to Dr. H. P. Wekesser on March 20, 1922.

5. Quoted in a letter sent by Mr. Page to Mr. John W. Miller on January 18, 1922.

6. Walter Duranty, op. cit., 103.

BIBLIOGRAPHY

Original Sources

1. Files of the Volga Relief Society.
2. All correspondence sent to Mr. and Mrs. George Repp and to Mr. John W. Miller between the years 1921-1926.
3. Files of the Central States Volga Relief Society.
4. Minute Book of the American Volga Relief Society, G. F. Schmidt, Secretary.

Periodicals

1. Literary Digest for the year 1921.
2. Die Welt Post for the year 1923.

Books

1. American Relief Administration Bulletin, Series 2, No. 42, November 1923. Sidney Brooks, "Russian Railroads in the National Crisis."
2. American Relief Administration Bulletin, Series 2, No. 43, December 1923. "The Carriage of Philanthropy" by "One who served".
3. Beratz, Gottlieb. Die deutschen Kolonien an der unteren Wolga in ihrer Entstehung und ersten Entwicklung. Saratow: H. Schellhorn und Co., 1915.
4. Bonwetsch, Gerhard. Geschichte der deutschen Kolonien an der Wolga. Stuttgart: Verlag von J. Engelhorns Nachf., 1919.
5. Duranty, Walter. I Write as I Please. New York: Simon and Schuster, 1935.

6. Fisher, H. H. **The Famine in Soviet Russian 1919-1923.** New York: The McMillan Company, 1927.

7. Golder, Frank A. and Lincoln Hutchinson. **On the Trail of the Russian Famine.** Stanford University, California: Stanford University Press, 1927.

8. Hoffmann, Hermann. "Auswanderung nach Russland im Jahre 1766." **Mitteilungen der hessischen familiengeschichtlichen Vereinigung.** Darmstadt, Januar 1927.

9. **Jahrbuch des Deutschtums im Ausland 1939.** "Der Wanderweg der Russlanddeutschen." Stuttgart: Deutsches Ausland Institut, 1939.

10. Sallet, Richard. "Russlanddeutsche Siedlungen in den Vereinigten Staaten." Vol. XXXI of **Jahrbuch der Deutsch-Amerikanischen Historischen Gesellschaft von Illinois.** Chicago, Ill.: The University of Chicago Press, 1931.

11. Schleuning, Johannes. **Aus tiefster Not.** Berlin, 1922.

12. Schleuning, Johannes. **Die deutschen Kolonien im Wolgagebiet.** Portland, Oregon, 1921.

13. Schmidt, G. F. **Bericht der American Volga Relief Society.** Lincoln, Nebraska, 1924.

14. Schwabenland, Emma D. "German-Russians on the Volga and in the United States." Unpublished M.A. Thesis, University of Colorado, 1929.

15. Surface, Frank M. and Raymond L. Bland. **American Food in the World War and Reconstruction Period.** Stanford University, California: Stanford University Press, 1931.